B"H

The Aishet Chayil is a selection of Mishlei that pays unique homage to the Jewish woman. King Solomon wrote this ode to the "lady of valor," praising her for her devotion.

This book is dedicated to all of the wonderful sisterhood we have as daughters of Yisrael.

May this treasure trove of verses give you support, encouragement, and inspiration always!

The Jewish Publication Society's The Holy Scriptures According to the Masoretic Text: A New Translation (1917) from the Public Domain.

תהלים
PSALMS

ספר ראשון
BOOK I

1Happy is the man that hath not walked in the counsel of the wicked,
Nor stood in the way of sinners,
Nor sat in the seat of the scornful.
2But his delight is in the law of the Lord;
And in His law doth he meditate day and night.
3And he shall be like a tree planted by streams of water,
That bringeth forth its fruit in its season,
And whose leaf doth not wither;
And in whatsoever he doeth he shall prosper.
4Not so the wicked;
But they are like the chaff which the wind driveth away,
5Therefore the wicked shall not stand in the judgment,
Nor sinners in the congregation of the righteous.
6For the LORD regardeth the way of the righteous,
But the way of the wicked shall perish.

2Why are the nations in an uproar?
And why do the peoples mutter in vain?
2The kings of the earth stand up,
And the rulers take counsel together,
Against the Lord, and against His anointed:
3'Let us break their bands asunder,
And cast away their cords from us.'
4He that sitteth in heaven laugheth,

The Lord hath them in derision.
⁵Then will He speak unto them in His wrath,
And affright them in His sore displeasure:
⁶'Truly it is I that have established My king
Upon Zion, My holy mountain.'
⁷I will tell of the decree:
The Lord said unto me: 'Thou art My son,
This day have I begotten thee.
⁸Ask of Me, and I will give the nations for thine inheritance,
And the ends of the earth for thy possession.
⁹Thou shalt break them with a rod of iron;
Thou shalt dash them in pieces like a potter's vessel.'
¹⁰Now therefore, ye kings, be wise;
Be admonished, ye judges of the earth.
¹¹Serve the LORD with fear,
And rejoice with trembling.
¹²Do homage in purity, lest He be angry, and ye perish in the way,
When suddenly His wrath is kindled.
Happy are all they that take refuge in Him.
3A Psalm of David, when he fled from Absalom his son.

²Lord, how many are mine adversaries become!
Many are they that rise up against me.
³Many there are that say of my soul:
'There is no salvation for him in God.'Selah
⁴But thou, O Lord, art a shield about me;
My glory, and the lifter up of my head.
⁵With my voice I call unto the Lord,
And He answereth me out of His holy mountain.Selah
⁶I lay me down, and I sleep;
I awake, for the Lord sustaineth me.
⁷I am not afraid of ten thousands of people,
That have set themselves against me round about.
⁸Arise, O Lord; save me, O my God;
For Thou hast smitten all mine enemies upon the cheek,
Thou hast broken the teeth of the wicked.
⁹Salvation belongeth unto the Lord;
Thy blessing be upon Thy people.Selah

4For the Leader; with string-music. A Psalm of David.

²Answer me when I call, O God of my righteousness,
Thou who didst set me free when I was in distress;
Be gracious unto me, and hear my prayer.

³O ye sons of men, how long shall my glory be put to shame,
In that ye love vanity, and seek after falsehood?Selah
⁴But know that the Lord hath set apart the godly man as His own;
The Lord will hear when I call unto Him.
⁵Tremble, and sin not;
Commune with your own heart upon your bed, and be still.Selah
⁶Offer the sacrifices of righteousness,
And put your trust in the Lord.
⁷Many there are that say: 'Oh that we could see some good!'
Lord, lift Thou up the light of Thy countenance upon us.
⁸Thou hast put gladness in my heart,
More than when their corn and their wine increase.
⁹In peace will I both lay me down and sleep;
For Thou, Lord, makest me dwell alone in safety.

5For the Leader; upon the Nehiloth. A Psalm of David.

²Give ear to my words, O Lord, consider my meditation.
³Hearken unto the voice of my cry, my King, and my God;
For unto Thee do I pray.
⁴O Lord, in the morning shalt Thou hear my voice;
In the morning will I order my prayer unto Thee, and will look forward.
⁵For Thou art not a God that hath pleasure in wickedness;
Evil shall not sojourn with Thee.
⁶The boasters shall not stand in Thy sight;
Thou hatest all workers of iniquity.
⁷Thou destroyest them that speak falsehood;
The Lord abhorreth the man of blood and of deceit.
⁸But as for me, in the abundance of Thy lovingkindness will I come into Thy house;
I will bow down toward Thy holy temple in the fear of Thee.
⁹O Lord, lead me in Thy righteousness because of them that lie in wait for me;
Make Thy way straight before my face.
¹⁰For there is no sincerity in their mouth;
Their inward part is a yawning gulf,
Their throat is an open sepulchre;
They make smooth their tongue.
¹¹Hold them guilty, O God,
Let them fall by their own counsels;
Cast them down in the multitude of their transgressions;
For they have rebelled against Thee.
¹²So shall all those that take refuge in Thee rejoice,
They shall ever shout for joy,
And Thou shalt shelter them;
Let them also that love Thy name exult in Thee.

[13]For Thou dost bless the righteous;
O Lord, Thou dost encompass him with favour as with a shield.

6For the Leader; with string-music; on the Sheminith. A Psalm of David.

[2]O Lord, rebuke me not in Thine anger,
Neither chasten me in Thy wrath.
[3]Be gracious unto me, O Lord, for I languish away;[5]
Heal me, O Lord, for my bones are affrighted.
[4]My soul also is sore affrighted;
And Thou, O Lord, how long?
[5]Return, O Lord, deliver my soul;
Save me for Thy mercy's sake.
[6]For in death there is no remembrance of Thee;
In the nether-world who will give Thee thanks?
[7]I am weary with my groaning;
Every night make I my bed to swim;
I melt away my couch with my tears.
[8]Mine eye is dimmed because of vexation;
It waxeth old because of all mine adversaries.
[9]Depart from me, all ye workers of iniquity;
For the Lord hath heard the voice of my weeping.
[10]The Lord hath heard my supplication;
The Lord receiveth my prayer.
[11]All mine enemies shall be ashamed and sore affrighted;
They shall turn back, they shall be ashamed suddenly.

7Shiggaion of David, which he sang unto the Lord, concerning Cush a Benjamite.

[2]O Lord my God, in Thee have I taken refuge;
Save me from all them that pursue me, and deliver me;
[3]Lest he tear my soul like a lion,
Rending it in pieces, while there is none to deliver.
[4]O Lord my God, if I have done this;
If there be iniquity in my hands;
[5]If I have requited him that did evil unto me,
Or spoiled mine adversary unto emptiness;
[6]Let the enemy pursue my soul, and overtake it,
And tread my life down to the earth;
Yea, let him lay my glory in the dust.Selah
[7]Arise, O Lord, in Thine anger,
Lift up Thyself in indignation against mine adversaries;
Yea, awake for me at the judgment which Thou hast commanded.
[8]And let the congregation of the peoples compass Thee about,

And over them return Thou on high.
⁹O Lord, who ministerest judgment to the peoples,
Judge me, O Lord,
According to my righteousness, and according to mine integrity that is in me.
¹⁰Oh that a full measure of evil might come upon the wicked,
And that Thou wouldest establish the righteous;
For the righteous God trieth the heart and reins.
¹¹My shield is with God,
Who saveth the upright in heart.
¹²God is a righteous judge,
Yea, a God that hath indignation every day:
¹³If a man turn not, He will whet His sword,
He hath bent His bow, and made it ready;
¹⁴He hath also prepared for him the weapons of death,
Yea, His arrows which He made sharp.
¹⁵Behold, he travaileth with iniquity;
Yea, he conceiveth mischief, and bringeth forth falsehood.
¹⁶He hath digged a pit, and hollowed it,
And is fallen into the ditch which he made.
¹⁷His mischief shall return upon his own head,
And his violence shall come down upon his own pate.
¹⁸I will give thanks unto the Lord according to His righteousness;
And will sing praise to the name of the Lord Most High.

8For the Leader; upon the Gittith. A Psalm of David.

²O Lord, our Lord,
How glorious is Thy name in all the earth!
Whose majesty is rehearsed above the heavens.
³Out of the mouth of babes and sucklings hast Thou founded strength,
Because of Thine adversaries;
That Thou mightest still the enemy and the avenger.
⁴When I behold Thy heavens, the work of Thy fingers,
The moon and the stars, which Thou hast established;
⁵What is man, that Thou art mindful of him?
And the son of man, that Thou thinkest of him?
⁶Yet Thou hast made him but little lower than the angels,
And hast crowned him with glory and honour.
⁷Thou hast made him to have dominion over the works of Thy hands;
Thou hast put all things under His feet:
⁸Sheep and oxen, all of them,
Yea, and the beasts of the field;
⁹The fowl of the air, and the fish of the sea;
Whatsoever passeth through the paths of the seas.

¹⁰O Lord, our Lord,
How glorious is Thy name in all the earth!

9For the Leader; upon Muth-labben. A Psalm of David.

²I will give thanks unto the Lord with my whole heart;
I will tell of all Thy marvellous works.
³I will be glad and exult in Thee;
I will sing praise to Thy name, O Most High:
⁴When mine enemies are turned back,
They stumble and perish at Thy presence;
⁵For Thou hast maintained my right and my cause;
Thou sattest upon the throne as the righteous Judge.
⁶Thou hast rebuked the nations,
Thou hast destroyed the wicked,
Thou hast blotted out their name for ever and ever.
⁷O thou enemy, the waste places are come to an end for ever;
And the cities which thou didst uproot,
Their very memorial is perished.
⁸But the Lord is enthroned for ever;
He hath established His throne for judgment.
⁹And He will judge the world in righteousness,
He will minister judgment to the peoples with equity.
¹⁰The Lord also will be a high tower for the oppressed,
A high tower in times of trouble;
¹¹And they that know Thy name will put their trust in Thee;
For thou, Lord, hast not forsaken them that seek Thee.
¹²Sing praises to the Lord, who dwelleth in Zion;
Declare among the peoples His doings.
¹³For He that avengeth blood hath remembered them;
He hath not forgotten the cry of the humble.
¹⁴Be gracious unto me, O Lord,
Behold mine affliction at the hands of them that hate me;
Thou that liftest me up from the gates of death;
¹⁵That I may tell of all Thy praise in the gates of the daughter of Zion,
That I may rejoice in Thy salvation.
¹⁶The nations are sunk down in the pit that they made;
In the net which they hid is their own foot taken.
¹⁷The Lord hath made Himself known, He hath executed judgment,
The wicked is snared in the work of his own hands. Higgaion.Selah
¹⁸The wicked shall return to the nether-world,
Even all the nations that forget God.
¹⁹For the needy shall not alway be forgotten,
Nor the expectation of the poor perish for ever.

²⁰Arise, O Lord, let not man prevail;
Let the nations be judged in Thy sight.
²¹Set terror over them, O Lord;
Let the nations know they are but men.Selah

10Why standest Thou afar off, O Lord?
Why hidest Thou Thyself in times of trouble?
²Through the pride of the wicked the poor is hotly pursued,
They are taken in the devices that they have imagined.
³For the wicked boasteth of his heart's desire,
And the covetous vaunteth himself, though he contemn the Lord.
⁴The wicked, in the pride of his countenance [, saith]: 'He will not require';
All his thoughts are: 'There is no God.'
⁵His ways prosper at all times;
Thy judgments are far above out of his sight;
As for all his adversaries, he puffeth at them.
⁶He saith in his heart: 'I shall not be moved,
I who to all generations shall not be in adversity.'
⁷His mouth is full of cursing and deceit and oppression;
Under his tongue is mischief and iniquity.
⁸He sitteth in the lurking-places of the villages;
In secret places doth he slay the innocent;
His eyes are on the watch for the helpless.
⁹He lieth in wait in a secret place as a lion in his lair,
He lieth in wait to catch the poor;
He doth catch the poor, when he draweth him up in his net.
¹⁰He croucheth, he boweth down,
And the helpless fall into his mighty claws.
¹¹He hath said in his heart: 'God hath forgotten;
He hideth His face; He will never see.'
¹²Arise, O Lord; O God, lift up Thy hand;
Forget not the humble.
¹³Wherefore doth the wicked contemn God,
And say in his heart: 'Thou wilt not require'?
¹⁴Thou hast seen; for Thou beholdest trouble and vexation, to requite them with Thy hand;
Unto Thee the helpless committeth himself;
Thou hast been the helper of the fatherless.
¹⁵Break Thou the arm of the wicked;
And as for the evil man, search out his wickedness, till none be found.
¹⁶The Lord is King for ever and ever;
The nations are perished out of His land.
¹⁷Lord, Thou hast heard the desire of the humble:
Thou wilt direct their heart, Thou wilt cause Thine ear to attend;
¹⁸To right the fatherless and the oppressed,

That man who is of the earth may be terrible no more.

11For the Leader. [A Psalm] of David.

In the Lord have I taken refuge;
How say ye to my soul:
'Flee thou! to your mountain, ye birds'?
²For, lo, the wicked bend the bow,
They have made ready their arrow upon the string,
That they may shoot in darkness at the upright in heart.
³When the foundations are destroyed,
What hath the righteous wrought?
⁴The Lord is in His holy temple,
The Lord, His throne is in heaven;
His eyes behold, His eyelids try, the children of men.
⁵The Lord trieth the righteous;
But the wicked and him that loveth violence His soul hateth.
⁶Upon the wicked He will cause to rain coals;
Fire and brimstone and burning wind shall be the portion of their cup.
⁷For the Lord is righteous, He loveth righteousness;
The upright shall behold His face.

12For the Leader; on the Sheminith. A Psalm of David.

²Help, Lord; for the godly man ceaseth;
For the faithful fail from among the children of men.
³They speak falsehood every one with his neighbour;
With flattering lip, and with a double heart, do they speak.
⁴May the Lord cut off all flattering lips,
The tongue that speaketh proud things!
⁵Who have said: 'Our tongue will we make mighty;
Our lips are with us: who is lord over us?'
⁶'For the oppression of the poor, for the sighing of the needy,
Now will I arise', saith the Lord;
'I will set him in safety at whom they puff.'
⁷The words of the Lord are pure words,
As silver tried in a crucible on the earth, refined seven times.
⁸Thou wilt keep them, O Lord;
Thou wilt preserve us from this generation for ever.
⁹The wicked walk on every side,
When vileness is exalted among the sons of men.

13For the Leader. A Psalm of David.

²How long, O Lord, wilt Thou forget me for ever?
How long wilt Thou hide Thy face from me?
³How long shall I take counsel in my soul, having sorrow in my heart by day?
How long shall mine enemy be exalted over me?
⁴Behold Thou, and answer me, O Lord my God;
Lighten mine eyes, lest I sleep the sleep of death;
⁵Lest mine enemy say: 'I have prevailed against him';
Lest mine adversaries rejoice when I am moved.
⁶But as for me, in Thy mercy do I trust;
My heart shall rejoice in Thy salvation.
I will sing unto the Lord,
Because He hath dealt bountifully with me.

14For the Leader. [A Psalm] of David.

The fool hath said in his heart: 'There is no God';
They have dealt corruptly, they have done abominably;
There is none that doeth good.
²The Lord looked forth from heaven upon the children of men,
To see if there were any man of understanding, that did seek after God.
³They are all corrupt, they are together become impure;
There is none that doeth good, no, not one.
⁴'Shall not all the workers of iniquity know it,
Who eat up My people as they eat bread,
And call not upon the Lord?'
⁵There are they in great fear;
For God is with the righteous generation.
⁶Ye would put to shame the counsel of the poor,
But the Lord is his refuge.
⁷Oh that the salvation of Israel were come out of Zion!
When the Lord turneth the captivity of His people,
Let Jacob rejoice, let Israel be glad.

15A Psalm of David.

Lord, who shall sojourn in Thy tabernacle?
Who shall dwell upon Thy holy mountain?
²He that walketh uprightly, and worketh righteousness,
And speaketh truth in his heart;
³That hath no slander upon his tongue,
Nor doeth evil to his fellow,
Nor taketh up a reproach against his neighbour;
⁴In whose eyes a vile person is despised,
But he honoureth them that fear the Lord;

He that sweareth to his own hurt, and changeth not;
⁵He that putteth not out his money on interest,
Nor taketh a bribe against the innocent.
He that doeth these things shall never be moved.

16Michtam of David.

Keep me, O God; for I have taken refuge in Thee.
²I have said unto the Lord: 'Thou art my Lord;
I have no good but in Thee';
³As for the holy that are in the earth,
They are the excellent in whom is all my delight.
⁴Let the idols of them be multiplied that make suit unto another;
Their drink-offerings of blood will I not offer,
Nor take their names upon my lips.
⁵O Lord, the portion of mine inheritance and of my cup,
Thou maintainest my lot.
⁶The lines are fallen unto me in pleasant places;
Yea, I have a goodly heritage.
⁷I will bless the Lord, who hath given me counsel;
Yea, in the night seasons my reins instruct me.
⁸I have set the Lord always before me;
Surely He is at my right hand, I shall not be moved.
⁹Therefore my heart is glad, and my glory rejoiceth;
My flesh also dwelleth in safety;
¹⁰For Thou wilt not abandon my soul to the nether-world;
Neither wilt Thou suffer Thy godly one to see the pit.
¹¹Thou makest me to know the path of life;
In Thy presence is fulness of joy,
In Thy right hand bliss for evermore.

17A Prayer of David.

Hear the right, O Lord, attend unto my cry;
Give ear unto my prayer from lips without deceit.
²Let my judgment come forth from Thy presence;
Let Thine eyes behold equity.
³Thou hast tried my heart, Thou hast visited it in the night;
Thou hast tested me, and Thou findest not
That I had a thought which should not pass my mouth.
⁴As for the doings of men, by the word of Thy lips
I have kept me from the ways of the violent.
⁵My steps have held fast to Thy paths,
My feet have not slipped.

⁶As for me, I call upon Thee, for Thou wilt answer me, O God;
Incline Thine ear unto me, hear my speech.
⁷Make passing great Thy mercies, O Thou that savest by Thy right hand
From assailants them that take refuge in Thee.
⁸Keep me as the apple of the eye,
Hide me in the shadow of Thy wings,
⁹From the wicked that oppress,
My deadly enemies, that compass me about.
¹⁰Their gross heart they have shut tight,
With their mouth they speak proudly.
¹¹At our every step they have now encompassed us;
They set their eyes to cast us down to the earth.
¹²He is like a lion that is eager to tear in pieces,
And like a young lion lurking in secret places.
¹³Arise, O Lord, confront him, cast him down;
Deliver my soul from the wicked, by Thy sword;
¹⁴From men, by Thy hand, O Lord,
From men of the world, whose portion is in this life,
And whose belly Thou fillest with Thy treasure;
Who have children in plenty,
And leave their abundance to their babes.
¹⁵As for me, I shall behold Thy face in righteousness;
I shall be satisfied, when I awake, with Thy likeness.

18For the Leader. [A Psalm] of David the servant of the Lord, who spoke unto the Lord the
words of this song in the day that the Lord delivered him from the hand of all his enemies, and
from the hand of Saul; ²And he said:
I love thee, O Lord, my strength.
³The Lord is my rock, and my fortress, and my deliverer;
My God, my rock, in Him I take refuge;
My shield, and my horn of salvation, my high tower.
⁴Praised, I cry, is the Lord,
And I am saved from mine enemies.
⁵The cords of Death compassed me,
And the floods of [1]Belial assailed me.
⁶The cords of [1]Sheol surrounded me;
The snares of Death confronted me.
⁷In my distress I called upon the Lord,
And cried unto my God;
Out of His temple He heard my voice,
And my cry came before Him unto His ears.
⁸Then the earth did shake and quake,
The foundations also of the mountains did tremble;
They were shaken, because He was wroth.

⁹Smoke arose up in His nostrils,
And fire out of His mouth did devour;
Coals flamed forth from Him.
¹⁰He bowed the heavens also, and came down;
And thick darkness was under His feet.
¹¹And He rode upon a cherub, and did fly;
Yea, He did swoop down upon the wings of the wind.
¹²He made darkness His hiding-place, His pavilion round about Him;
Darkness of waters, thick clouds of the skies.
¹³At the brightness before Him, there passed through His thick clouds
Hailstones and coals of fire.
¹⁴The Lord also thundered in the heavens,
And the Most High gave forth His voice;
Hailstones and coals of fire.
¹⁵And He sent out His arrows, and scattered them;
And He shot forth lightnings, and discomfited them.
¹⁶And the channels of waters appeared,
And the foundations of the world were laid bare,
At Thy rebuke, O Lord,
At the blast of the breath of Thy nostrils.
¹⁷He sent from on high, He took me;
He drew me out of many waters.
¹⁸He delivered me from mine enemy
most strong,
And from them that hated me, for they were too mighty for me.
¹⁹They confronted me in the day of my calamity;
But the Lord was a stay unto me.
²⁰He brought me forth also into a large place;
He delivered me, because He delighted in me.
²¹The Lord rewarded me according to my righteousness;
According to the cleanness of my hands hath He recompensed me.
²²For I have kept the ways of the Lord,
And have not wickedly departed from my God.
²³For all His ordinances were before me,
And I put not away His statutes from me.
²⁴And I was single-hearted with Him,
And I kept myself from mine iniquity.
²⁵Therefore hath the Lord recompensed me according to my righteousness,
According to the cleanness of my hands in His eyes.
²⁶With the merciful Thou dost show Thyself merciful,
With the upright man Thou dost show Thyself upright;
²⁷With the pure Thou dost show Thyself pure;
And with the crooked Thou dost show Thyself subtle.
²⁸For Thou dost save the afflicted people;

But the haughty eyes Thou dost humble.
29For Thou dost light my lamp;
The Lord my God doth lighten my darkness.
30For by Thee I run upon a troop;
And by my God do I scale a wall.
31As for God, His way is perfect;
The word of the Lord is tried;
He is a shield unto all them that take refuge in Him.
32For who is God, save the Lord?
And who is a Rock, except our God?
33The God that girdeth me with strength,
And maketh my way straight;
34Who maketh my feet like hinds',
And setteth me upon my high places;
35Who traineth my hands for war,
So that mine arms do bend a bow of brass.
36Thou hast also given me Thy shield of salvation,
And Thy right hand hath holden me up;
And Thy condescension hath made me great.
37Thou hast enlarged my steps under me,
And my feet have not slipped.
38I have pursued mine enemies, and overtaken them;
Neither did I turn back till they were consumed.
39I have smitten them through, so that they are not able to rise;
They are fallen under my feet.
40For Thou hast girded me with strength unto the battle;
Thou hast subdued under me those that rose up against me.
41Thou hast also made mine enemies turn their backs unto me,
And I did cut off them that hate me.
42They cried, but there was none to save;
Even unto the Lord, but He answered them not.
43Then did I beat them small as the dust before the wind;
I did cast them out as the mire of the streets.
44Thou hast delivered me from the contentions of the people;
Thou hast made me the head of the nations;
A people whom I have not known serve me.
45As soon as they hear of me, they obey me;
The sons of the stranger dwindle away before me.
46The sons of the stranger fade away,
And come trembling out of their close places.
47The Lord liveth, and blessed be my Rock;
And exalted be the God of my salvation;
48Even the God that executeth vengeance for me,
And subdueth peoples under me.

⁴⁹He delivereth me from mine enemies;
Yea, Thou liftest me up above them that rise up against me;
Thou deliverest me from the violent man.
⁵⁰Therefore I will give thanks unto Thee, O Lord, among the nations,
And will sing praises unto Thy name.
⁵¹Great salvation giveth He to His king;
And showeth mercy to His anointed,
To David and to his seed, for evermore.

19 For the Leader. A Psalm of David.

²The heavens declare the glory of God,
And the firmament showeth His handiwork;
³Day unto day uttereth speech,
And night unto night revealeth knowledge;
⁴There is no speech, there are no words,
Neither is their voice heard.
⁵Their line is gone out through all the earth,
And their words to the end of the world.
In them hath He set a tent for the sun,
⁶Which is as a bridegroom coming out of his chamber,
And rejoiceth as a strong man to run his course.
⁷His going forth is from the end of the heaven,
And his circuit unto the ends of it;
And there is nothing hid from the heat thereof.
⁸The law of the Lord is perfect, restoring the soul;
The testimony of the Lord is sure, making wise the simple.
⁹The precepts of the Lord are right, rejoicing the heart;
The commandment of the Lord is pure, enlightening the eyes.
¹⁰The fear of the Lord is clean, enduring for ever;
The ordinances of the Lord are true, they are righteous altogether;
¹¹More to be desired are they than gold, yea, than much fine gold;
Sweeter also than honey and the honeycomb.
¹²Moreover by them is Thy servant warned;
In keeping of them there is great reward.
¹³Who can discern his errors?
Clear Thou me from hidden faults.
¹⁴Keep back Thy servant also from presumptuous sins,
That they may not have dominion over me; then shall I be faultless,
And I shall be clear from great transgression.
¹⁵Let the words of my mouth and the meditation of my heart be acceptable before Thee,
O Lord, my Rock, and my Redeemer.

20 For the Leader. A Psalm of David.

²The Lord answer thee in the day of trouble;
The name of the God of Jacob set thee up on high;
³Send forth thy help from the sanctuary,
And support thee out of Zion;
⁴Receive the memorial of all thy meal-offerings,
And accept the fat of thy burnt-sacrifice;Selah
⁵Grant thee according to thine own heart,
And fulfil all thy counsel.
⁶We will shout for joy in thy victory,
And in the name of our God we will set up our standards;
The Lord fulfil all thy petitions.
⁷Now know I that the Lord saveth His anointed;
He will answer him from His holy heaven
With the mighty acts of His saving right hand.
⁸Some trust in chariots, and some in horses;
But we will make mention of the name of the Lord our God.
⁹They are bowed down and fallen;
But we are risen, and stand upright.
¹⁰Save, Lord;
Let the King answer us in the day that we call.

21For the Leader. A Psalm of David.
²O Lord, in Thy strength the king rejoiceth;
And in Thy salvation how greatly doth he exult!
³Thou hast given him his heart's desire,
And the request of his lips Thou hast not withholden.Selah
⁴For Thou meetest him with choicest blessings;
Thou settest a crown of fine gold on his head.
⁵He asked life of Thee, Thou gavest it him;
Even length of days for ever and ever.
⁶His glory is great through Thy salvation;
Honour and majesty dost Thou lay upon him.
⁷For Thou makest him most blessed for ever;
Thou makest Mm glad with joy in Thy presence.
⁸For the king trusteth in the Lord,
Yea, in the mercy of the Most High; he shall not be moved.
⁹Thy hand shall be equal to all thine enemies;
Thy right hand shall overtake those that hate thee.
¹⁰Thou shalt make them as a fiery furnace in the time of thine anger;
The Lord shall swallow them up in His wrath,
And the fire shall devour them.
¹¹Their fruit shalt thou destroy from the earth,
And their seed from among the children of men.

¹²For they intended evil against thee,
They imagined a device, wherewith they shall not prevail.
¹³For thou shalt make them turn their back,
Thou shalt make ready with thy bowstrings against the face of them.
¹⁴Be Thou exalted, O Lord, in Thy strength;
So will we sing and praise Thy power.

22For the Leader; upon Aijeleth ha-Shahar. A Psalm of David.
²My God, my God, why hast Thou forsaken me,
And art far from my help at the words of my cry?
³O my God, I call by day, but Thou answerest not;
And at night, and there is no surcease for me.
⁴Yet Thou art holy,
Thou that art enthroned upon the praises of Israel.
⁵In Thee did our fathers trust;
They trusted, and Thou didst deliver them.
⁶Unto Thee they cried, and escaped;
In Thee did they trust, and were not ashamed.
⁷But I am a worm, and no man,
A reproach of men, and despised of the people.
⁸All they that see me laugh me to scorn,
They shoot out the lip, they shake the head:
⁹'Let him commit himself unto the Lord! let Him rescue him;
Let Him deliver him, seeing He delighteth in him.'
¹⁰For Thou art He that took me out of the womb,
Thou madest me trust when I was upon my mother's breasts.
¹¹Upon Thee I have been cast from my birth;
Thou art my God from my mother's womb.
¹²Be not far from me; for trouble is near;
For there is none to help.
¹³Many bulls have encompassed me;
Strong bulls of Bashan have beset me round.
¹⁴They open wide their mouth against me,
As a ravening and a roaring lion.
¹⁵I am poured out like water,
And all my bones are out of joint;
My heart is become like wax;
It is melted in mine inmost parts
¹⁶My strength is dried up like a potsherd;
And my tongue cleaveth to my throat;
And Thou layest me in the dust of death.
¹⁷For dogs have encompassed me,
A company of evil-doers have inclosed me;
Like a lion, they are at my hands and my feet.

¹⁸I may count all my bones;
They look and gloat over me.
¹⁹They part my garments among them,
And for my vesture do they cast lots.
²⁰But Thou, Lord, be not far off;
Thou my strength, hasten to help me.
²¹Deliver my soul from the sword;
Mine only one from the power of the dog.
²²Save me from the lion's mouth;
Yea, from the horns of the wild-oxen do Thou answer me.
²³I will declare Thy name unto my brethren;
In the midst of the congregation will I praise Thee:
²⁴'Ye that fear the Lord, praise Him;
All ye the seed of Jacob, glorify Him;
And stand in awe of Him, all ye the seed of Israel.
²⁵For He hath not despised nor abhorred the lowliness of the poor;
Neither hath He hid His face from him;
But when he cried unto Him, He heard.'
²⁶From Thee cometh my praise in the great congregation,
I will pay my vows before them that fear Him.
²⁷Let the humble eat and be satisfied;
Let them praise the Lord that seek after Him;
May your heart be quickened for ever!
²⁸All the ends of the earth shall remember and turn unto the Lord;
And all the kindreds of the nations shall worship before Thee.
²⁹For the kingdom is the Lord's;
And He is the ruler over the nations.
³⁰All the fat ones of the earth shall eat and worship;
All they that go down to the dust shall kneel before Him,
Even he that cannot keep his soul alive.
³¹A seed shall serve him,
It shall be told of the Lord unto the next generation.
³²They shall come and shall declare His righteousness
Unto a people that shall be born, that He hath done it.

23 A Psalm of David.
The Lord is my shepherd; I shall not want.
²He maketh me to lie down in green pastures;
He leadeth me beside the still waters.
³He restoreth my soul;
He guideth me in straight paths for His name's sake.
⁴Yea, though I walk through the valley of the shadow of death,
I will fear no evil,
For Thou art with me;

Thy rod and Thy staff, they comfort me.
⁵Thou preparest a table before me in the presence of mine enemies;
Thou hast anointed my head with oil; my cup runneth over.
⁶Surely goodness and mercy shall follow me all the days of my life;
And I shall dwell in the house of the Lord for ever.

24A Psalm of David.
The earth is the Lord's, and the fulness thereof;
The world, and they that dwell therein.
²For He hath founded it upon the seas,
And established it upon the floods.
³Who shall ascend into the mountain of the Lord?
And who shall stand in His holy place?
⁴He that hath clean hands, and a pure heart;
Who hath not taken My name in vain,
And hath not sworn deceitfully
⁵He shall receive a blessing from the Lord,
And righteousness from the God of his salvation.
⁶Such is the generation of them that seek after Him,
That seek Thy face, even Jacob.
Selah
⁷Lift up your heads, O ye gates,
And be ye lifted up, ye everlasting doors;
That the King of glory may come in.
⁸'Who is the King of glory?'
'The Lord strong and mighty,
The Lord mighty in battle.'
⁹Lift up your heads, O ye gates,
Yea, lift them up, ye everlasting doors;
That the King of glory may come in.
¹⁰'Who then is the King of glory?'
'The Lord of hosts;
He is the King of glory.'Selah

25[A Psalm] of David.
אUnto Thee, O Lord, do I lift up my soul.
²בO my God, in Thee have I trusted, let me not be ashamed;
Let not mine enemies triumph over me.
³גYea, none that wait for Thee shall be ashamed;
They shall be ashamed that deal treacherously without cause.
⁴דShow me Thy ways, O Lord;
Teach me Thy paths.
⁵הוGuide me in Thy truth, and teach me;
For Thou art the God of my salvation;

For Thee do I wait all the day.
[6]דRemember, O Lord, Thy compassions and Thy mercies;
For they have been from of old.
[7]נRemember not the sins of my youth, nor my transgressions;
According to Thy mercy remember Thou me,
For thy goodness' sake, O Lord.
[8]טGood and upright is the Lord;
Therefore doth He instruct sinners in the way.
[9]יHe guideth the humble in justice;
And He teacheth the humble His way.
[10]כAll the paths of the Lord are mercy and truth
Unto such as keep His covenant and His testimonies.
[11]לFor Thy name's sake, O Lord,
Pardon mine iniquity, for it is great,
[12]מWhat man is he that feareth the Lord?
Him will He instruct in the way that he should choose.
[13]נHis soul shall abide in prosperity,
And his seed shall inherit the land.
[14]סThe counsel of the Lord is with them that fear Him;
And His covenant, to make them know it.
[15]עMine eyes are ever toward the Lord;
For He will bring forth my feet out of the net.
[16]פTurn Thee unto me, and be gracious unto me;
For I am solitary and afflicted.
[17]צThe troubles of my heart are enlarged;
O bring Thou me out of my distresses.
[18]רSee mine affliction and my travail;
And forgive all my sins.
[19]Consider how many are mine enemies,
And the cruel hatred wherewith they hate me.
[20]שO keep my soul, and deliver me;
Let me not be ashamed, for I have taken refuge in Thee.
[21]תLet integrity and uprightness preserve me;
Because I wait for Thee.
[22]Redeem Israel, O God,
Out of all his troubles.

26[A Psalm] of David.
Judge me, O Lord, for I have walked in mine integrity,
And I have trusted in the Lord without wavering.
[2]Examine me, O Lord, and try me,
Test my reins and my heart.
[3]For Thy mercy is before mine eyes;
And I have walked in Thy truth.

[4]I have not sat with men of falsehood;
Neither will I go in with dissemblers.
[5]I hate the gathering of evil-doers,
And will not sit with the wicked
[6]I will wash my hands in innocency;
So will I compass Thine altar, O Lord,
[7]That I may make the voice of thanksgiving to be heard,
And tell of all Thy wondrous works.
[8]Lord, I love the habitation of Thy house,
And the place where Thy glory dwelleth.
[9]Gather not my soul with sinners,
Nor my life with men of blood;
[10]In whose hands is craftiness,
And their right hand is full of bribes.
[11]But as for me, I will walk in mine integrity;
Redeem me, and be gracious unto me.
[12]My foot standeth in an even place;
In the congregations will I bless the Lord.

27[A Psalm] of David.

The Lord is my light and my salvation; whom shall I fear?
The Lord is the stronghold of my life; of whom shall I be afraid?
[2]When evil-doers came upon me to eat up my flesh,
Even mine adversaries and my foes, they stumbled and fell.
[3]Though a host should encamp against me,
My heart shall not fear;
Though war should rise up against me,
Even then will I be confident.
[4]One thing have I asked of the Lord, that will I seek after:
That I may dwell in the house of the Lord all the days of my life,
To behold the graciousness of the Lord, and to visit early in His temple.
[5]For He concealeth me in His pavilion in the day of evil;
He hideth me in the covert of His tent;
He lifteth me up upon a rock.
[6]And now shall my head be lifted up above mine enemies round about me;
And I will offer in His tabernacle sacrifices with trumpet-sound;
I will sing, yea, I will sing praises unto the Lord.
[7]Hear, O Lord, when I call with my voice,
And be gracious unto me, and answer me.
[8]In Thy behalf my heart hath said: 'Seek ye My face';
Thy face, Lord, will I seek.
[9]Hide not Thy face far from me;
Put not Thy servant away in anger;

Thou hast been my help;
Cast me not off, neither forsake me, O God of my salvation.
[10]For though my father and my mother have forsaken me,
The Lord will take me up.
[11]Teach me Thy way, O Lord;
And lead me in an even path,
Because of them that lie in wait for me.
[12]Deliver me not over unto the will of mine adversaries;
For false witnesses are risen up against me, and such as breathe out violence.
[13]If I had not believed to look upon the goodness of the Lord
In the land of the living!—
[14]Wait on the Lord;
Be strong, and let thy heart take courage;
Yea, wait thou for the Lord.

28[A Psalm] of David.

Unto thee, O Lord, do I call;
My Rock, be not Thou deaf unto me;
Lest, if Thou be silent unto me,
I become like them that go down into the pit.
[2]Hear the voice of my supplications, when I cry unto Thee,
When I lift up my hands toward Thy holy Sanctuary.
[3]Draw me not away with the wicked,
And with the workers of iniquity;
Who speak peace with their neighbours,
But evil is in their hearts.
[4]Give them according to their deeds, and according to the evil of their endeavours;
Give them after the work of their hands;
Render to them their desert.
[5]Because they give no heed to the works of the Lord,
Nor to the operation of His hands;
He will break them down and not build them up.
[6]Blessed be the Lord,
Because He hath heard the voice of my supplications.
[7]The Lord is my strength and my shield,
In Him hath my heart trusted, And I am helped;
Therefore my heart greatly rejoiceth,
And with my song will I praise Him.
[8]The Lord is a strength unto them;
And He is a stronghold of salvation to His anointed.
[9]Save Thy people, and bless Thine inheritance;
And tend them, and carry them for ever.

29A Psalm of David.

Ascribe unto the Lord, O ye sons of might,
Ascribe unto the Lord glory and strength.
²Ascribe unto the Lord the glory due unto His name;
Worship the Lord in the beauty of holiness.
³The voice of the Lord is upon the waters;
The God of glory thundereth,
Even the Lord upon many waters.
⁴The voice of the Lord is powerful;
The voice of the Lord is full of majesty.
⁵The voice of the Lord breaketh the cedars;
Yea, the Lord breaketh in pieces the cedars of Lebanon.
⁶He maketh them also to skip like a calf;
Lebanon and Sirion like a young wild-ox.
⁷The voice of the Lord heweth out flames of fire.
⁸The voice of the Lord shaketh the wilderness;
The Lord shaketh the wilderness of Kadesh.
⁹The voice of the Lord maketh the hinds to calve,
And strippeth the forests bare;
And in His temple all say: 'Glory.'
¹⁰The Lord sat enthroned at the flood;
Yea, the Lord sitteth as King for ever.
¹¹The Lord will give strength unto His people;
The Lord will bless his people with peace.

30A Psalm; a Song at the Dedication of the House; of David.

²I will extol thee, O Lord, for Thou hast raised me up,
And hast not suffered mine enemies to rejoice over me.
³O Lord my God,
I cried unto Thee, and Thou didst heal me;
⁴O Lord, Thou broughtest up my soul from the nether-world;
Thou didst kept me alive, that I should not go down to the pit.
⁵Sing praise unto the Lord, O ye His godly ones,
And give thanks to His holy name.
⁶For His anger is but for a moment,²⁹
His favour is for a life-time;
Weeping may tarry for the night,
But joy cometh in the morning.
⁷Now I had said in my security: '
I shall never be moved.'
⁸Thou hadst established, O Lord, in Thy favour my mountain as a stronghold—
Thou didst hide Thy face; I was affrighted.

⁹Unto Thee, O Lord, did I call,
And unto the Lord I made supplication:
¹⁰'What profit is there in my blood, when I go down to the pit?
Shall the dust praise Thee? shall it declare Thy truth?
¹¹Hear, O Lord, and be gracious unto me;
Lord, be Thou my helper.'
¹²Thou didst turn for me my mourning into dancing;
Thou didst loose my sackcloth, and gird me with gladness;
¹³So that my glory may sing praise to Thee, and not be silent;
O Lord my God, I will give thanks unto Thee for ever.

31 For the Leader. A Psalm of David.

²In thee, O Lord, have I taken refuge; let me never be ashamed;
Deliver me in Thy righteousness.
³Incline Thine ear unto me, deliver me speedily;
Be Thou to me a rock of refuge, even a fortress of defence, to save me.
⁴For Thou art my rock and my fortress;
Therefore for Thy name's sake lead me and guide me.
⁵Bring me forth out of the net that they have hidden for me;
For Thou art my stronghold.
⁶Into Thy hand I commit my spirit;
Thou hast redeemed me, O Lord, Thou God of truth.
⁷I hate them that regard lying vanities;
But I trust in the Lord.
⁸I will be glad and rejoice in Thy lovingkindness;
For Thou hast seen mine affliction,
Thou hast taken cognizance of the troubles of my soul,
⁹And Thou hast not given me over into the hand of the enemy;
Thou hast set my feet in a broad place.
¹⁰Be gracious unto me, O Lord, for I am in distress;
Mine eye wasteth away with vexation, yea, my soul and my body.
¹¹For my life is spent in sorrow, and my years in sighing;
My strength faileth because of mine iniquity, and my bones are wasted away.
¹²Because of all mine adversaries I am become a reproach,
Yea, unto my neighbours exceedingly, and a dread to mine acquaintance;
They that see me without flee from me.
¹³I am forgotten as a dead man out of mind;
I am like a useless vessel.
¹⁴For I have heard the whispering of many,
Terror on every side;
While they took counsel together against me,
They devised to take away my life.
¹⁵But as for me, I have trusted in Thee, O Lord;

I have said: 'Thou art my God.'

¹⁶My times are in Thy hand;

Deliver me from the hand of mine enemies, and from them that persecute me.

¹⁷Make Thy face to shine upon Thy servant;

Save me in Thy lovingkindness.

¹⁸O Lord, let me not be ashamed, for I have called upon Thee;

Let the wicked be ashamed, let them be put to silence in the nether-world.

¹⁹Let the lying lips be dumb,

Which speak arrogantly against the righteous,

With pride and contempt.

²⁰Oh how abundant is Thy goodness, which Thou hast laid up for them that fear Thee;

Which Thou hast wrought for them that take their refuge in Thee, in the sight of the sons of men!

²¹Thou hidest them in the covert of Thy presence from the plottings of man;

Thou concealest them in a pavilion from the strife of tongues.

²²Blessed be the Lord;

For He hath shown me His wondrous lovingkindness in an entrenched city.

²³As for me, I said in my haste: 'I am cut off from before Thine eyes';

Nevertheless Thou heardest the voice of my supplications when I cried unto Thee.

²⁴O love the Lord, all ye His godly ones;

The Lord preserveth the faithful,

And plentifully repayeth him that acteth haughtily.

²⁵Be strong, and let your heart take courage,

All ye that wait for the Lord.

32[A Psalm] of David. Maschil.

Happy is he whose transgression is forgiven, whose sin is pardoned.

²Happy is the man unto whom the Lord counteth not iniquity,

And in whose spirit there is no guile.

³When I kept silence, my bones wore away Through my groaning all the day long.

⁴For day and night Thy hand was heavy upon me;

My sap was turned as in the droughts of summer.Selah

⁵I acknowledged my sin unto Thee, and mine iniquity have I not hid;

I said: 'I will make confession concerning my transgressions unto the Lord'—

And Thou, Thou forgavest the iniquity of my sin.Selah

⁶For this let every one that is godly pray unto Thee in a time when Thou mayest be found;

Surely, when the great waters overflow, they will not reach unto him.

⁷Thou art my hiding-place; Thou wilt preserve me from the adversary;

With songs of deliverance Thou wilt compass me about.Selah

⁸'I will instruct thee and teach thee in the way which thou shalt go;

I will give counsel, Mine eye being upon thee.'

⁹Be ye not as the horse, or as the mule, which have no understanding;

Whose mouth must be held in with bit and bridle,

That they come not near unto thee.

¹⁰Many are the sorrows of the wicked;
But he that trusteth in the Lord, mercy compasseth him about.
¹¹Be glad in the Lord, and rejoice, ye righteous;
And shout for joy, all ye that are upright in heart.

33Rejoice in the Lord, O ye righteous,
Praise is comely for the upright.
²Give thanks unto the Lord with harp,
Sing praises unto Him with the psaltery of ten strings.
³Sing unto Him a new song;
Play skilfully amid shouts of joy.
⁴For the word of the Lord is upright;
And all His work is done in faithfulness.
⁵He loveth righteousness and justice;
The earth is full of the lovingkindness of the Lord.
⁶By the word of the Lord were the heavens made;
And all the host of them by the breath of His mouth.
⁷He gathereth the waters of the sea together as a heap;
He layeth up the deeps in store-houses.
⁸Let all the earth fear the Lord;
Let all the inhabitants of the world stand in awe of Him.
⁹For He spoke, and it was;
He commanded, and it stood.
¹⁰The Lord bringeth the counsel of the nations to nought;
He maketh the thoughts of the peoples to be of no effect.
¹¹The counsel of the Lord standeth for ever,
The thoughts of His heart to all generations.
¹²Happy is the nation whose God is the Lord;
The people whom He hath chosen for His own inheritance.
¹³The Lord looketh from heaven;
He beholdeth all the sons of men;
¹⁴From the place of His habitation He looketh intently
Upon all the inhabitants of the earth;
¹⁵He that fashioneth the hearts of them all,
That considereth all their doings.
¹⁶A king is not saved by the multitude of a host;
A mighty man is not delivered by great strength.
¹⁷A horse is a vain thing for safety;
Neither doth it afford escape by its great strength.
¹⁸Behold, the eye of the Lord is toward them that fear Him,
Toward them that wait for His mercy;
¹⁹To deliver their soul from death,
And to keep them alive in famine.
²⁰Our soul hath waited for the Lord;

He is our help and our shield.
²¹For in Him doth our heart rejoice,
Because we have trusted in His holy name.
²²Let Thy mercy, O Lord, be upon us,
According as we have waited for Thee.

34[A Psalm] of David; when he changed his demeanour before Abimelech, who drove him away, and he departed.

²אI will bless the Lord at all times;
His praise shall continually be in my mouth.
³בMy soul shall glory in the Lord;
The humble shall hear thereof, and be glad.
⁴גO magnify the Lord with me,
And let us exalt His name together.
⁵דI sought the Lord, and He answered me,
And delivered me from all my fears.
⁶הThey looked unto Him, and were radiant;
וAnd their faces shall never be abashed.
⁷זThis poor man cried, and the Lord heard,
And saved him out of all his troubles.
⁸חThe angel of the Lord encampeth round about them that fear Him,
And delivereth them.
⁹טO consider and see that the Lord is good;
Happy is the man that taketh refuge in Him.
¹⁰יO fear the Lord, ye His holy ones;
For there is no want to them that fear Him.
¹¹כThe young lions do lack, and suffer hunger;
But they that seek the Lord want not any good thing.
¹²לCome, ye children, hearken unto me;
I will teach you the fear of the Lord.
¹³מWho is the man that desireth life,
And loveth days, that he may see good therein?
¹⁴נKeep thy tongue from evil,
And thy lips from speaking guile.
¹⁵סDepart from evil, and do good;
Seek peace, and pursue it.
¹⁶עThe eyes of the Lord are toward the righteous,
And His ears are open unto their cry.
¹⁷פThe face of the Lord is against them that do evil,
To cut off the remembrance of them from the earth.
²]¹⁸צ]They cried, and the Lord heard,
And delivered them out of all their troubles.
¹⁹קThe Lord is nigh unto them that are of a broken heart,

And saveth such as are of a contrite spirit.
20 רMany are the ills of the righteous,
But the Lord delivereth him out of them all.
21 שHe keepeth all his bones;
Not one of them is broken.
22 תEvil shall kill the wicked;
And they that hate the righteous shall be held guilty.
23 The Lord redeemeth the soul of His servants;
And none of them that take refuge in Him shall be desolate.

35[A Psalm] of David.

Strive, O Lord, with them that strive with me;
Fight against them that fight against me.
2 Take hold of shield and buckler,
And rise up to my help.
3 Draw out also the spear, and the battle-axe, against them that pursue me;
Say unto my soul: 'I am Thy salvation.'
4 Let them be ashamed and brought to confusion that seek after my soul;
Let them be turned back and be abashed that devise my hurt.
5 Let them be as chaff before the wind,
The angel of the Lord thrusting them.
6 Let their way be dark and slippery,
The angel of the Lord pursuing them.
7 For without cause have they hid for me the pit, even their net,
Without cause have they digged for my soul.
8 Let destruction come upon him unawares;
And let his net that he hath hid catch himself;
With destruction let him fall therein.
9 And my soul shall be joyful in the Lord;
It shall rejoice in His salvation.
10 All my bones shall say: 'Lord, who is like unto Thee,
Who deliverest the poor from him that is too strong for him,
Yea, the poor and the needy from him that spoileth him?'
11 Unrighteous witnesses rise up;
They ask me of things that I know not.
12 They repay me evil for good;
Bereavement is come to my soul.
13 But as for me, when they were sick, my clothing was sackcloth,
I afflicted my soul with fasting;
And my prayer, may it return into mine own bosom.
14 I went about as though it had been my friend or my brother;
I bowed down mournful, as one that mourneth for his mother.
15 But when I halt they rejoice, and gather themselves together;

The abjects gather themselves together against me, and those whom I know not;
They tear me, and cease not;
[16]With the profanest mockeries of backbiting
They gnash at me with their teeth.
[17]Lord, how long wilt Thou look on?
Rescue my soul from their destructions,
Mine only one from the lions.
[18]I will give Thee thanks in the great congregation;
I will praise Thee among a numerous people.
[19]Let not them that are wrongfully mine enemies rejoice over me;
Neither let them wink with the eye that hate me without a cause.
[20]For they speak not peace;
But they devise deceitful matters against them that are quiet in the land.
[21]Yea, they open their mouth wide against me;
They say: 'Aha, aha, our eye hath seen it.'
[22]Thou hast seen, O Lord; keep not silence;
O Lord, be not far from me.
[23]Rouse Thee, and awake to my judgment,
Even unto my cause, my God and my Lord.
[24]Judge me, O Lord my God, according to Thy righteousness;
And let them not rejoice over me.
[25]Let them not say in their heart: 'Aha, we have our desire';
Let them not say: 'We have swallowed him up.'
[26]Let them be ashamed and abashed together that rejoice at my hurt;
Let them be clothed with shame and confusion that magnify themselves against me.
[27]Let them shout for joy, and be glad, that delight in my righteousness;
Yea, let them say continually: 'Magnified be the Lord,
Who delighteth in the peace of His servant.'
[28]And my tongue shall speak of Thy righteousness,
And of Thy praise all the day.

36For the Leader. [A Psalm] of David the servant of the Lord

[2]Transgression speaketh to the wicked, methinks—
There is no fear of God before his eyes.
[3]For it flattereth him in his eyes,
Until his iniquity be found, and he be hated.
[4]The words of his mouth are iniquity and deceit;
He hath left off to be wise, to do good.
[5]He deviseth iniquity upon his bed;
He setteth himself in a way that is not good;
He abhorreth not evil.
[6]Thy lovingkindness, O Lord, is in the heavens;
Thy faithfulness reacheth unto the skies.

[7]Thy righteousness is like the mighty mountains;
Thy judgments are like the great deep;
Man and beast Thou preservest, O Lord.
[8]How precious is Thy lovingkindness, O God!
And the children of men take refuge in the shadow of Thy wings.
[9]They are abundantly satisfied with the fatness of Thy house;
And Thou makest them drink of the river of Thy pleasures.
[10]For with Thee is the fountain of life;
In Thy light do we see light.
[11]O continue Thy lovingkindness unto them that know Thee;
And Thy righteousness to the upright in heart.
[12]Let not the foot of pride overtake me,
And let not the hand of the wicked drive me away.
[13]There are the workers of iniquity fallen;
They are thrust down, and are not able to rise.

37[A Psalm] of David.

אFret not thyself because of evil-doers,
Neither be thou envious against them that work unrighteousness.
[2]For they shall soon wither like the grass,
And fade as the green herb.
[3]בTrust in the Lord, and do good;
Dwell in the land, and cherish faithfulness.
[4]So shalt thou delight thyself in the Lord;
And He shall give thee the petitions of thy heart.
[5]גCommit thy way unto the Lord;
Trust also in Him, and He will bring it to pass.
[6]And He will make thy righteousness to go forth as the light,
And thy right as the noonday.
[7]דResign thyself unto the Lord, and wait patiently for Him;
Fret not thyself because of him who prospereth in his way,
Because of the man who bringeth wicked devices to pass.
[8]הCease from anger, and forsake wrath;
Fret not thyself, it tendeth only to evil-doing.
[9]For evil-doers shall be cut off;
But those that wait for the Lord, they shall inherit the land.
[10]וAnd yet a little while, and the wicked is no more;
Yea, thou shalt look well at his place, and he is not.
[11]But the humble shall inherit the land,
And delight themselves in the abundance of peace.
[12]זThe wicked plotteth against the righteous,
And gnasheth at him with his teeth.
[13]The Lord doth laugh at him;

For He seeth that his day is coming.

14 נThe wicked have drawn out the sword, and have bent their bow;
To cast down the poor and needy,
To slay such as are upright in the way;

15 Their sword shall enter into their own heart,
And their bows shall be broken.

16 סBetter is a little that the righteous hath
Than the abundance of many wicked.

17 For the arms of the wicked shall be broken;
But the Lord upholdeth the righteous.

18 עThe Lord knoweth the days of them that are whole-hearted;
And their inheritance shall be for ever.

19 They shall not be ashamed in the time of evil;
And in the days of famine they shall be satisfied.

20 פFor the wicked shall perish,
And the enemies of the Lord shall be as the fat of lambs—
They shall pass away in smoke, they shall pass away.

21 לThe wicked borroweth, and payeth not;
But the righteous dealeth graciously, and giveth.

22 For such as are blessed of Him shall inherit the land;
And they that are cursed of Him shall be cut off.

23 מIt is of the Lord that a man's goings are established;
And He delighted in his way.

24 Though he fall, he shall not be utterly cast down;
For the Lord upholdeth his hand.

25 נI have been young, and now am old;
Yet have I not seen the righteous forsaken,
Nor his seed begging bread.

26 All the day long he dealeth graciously, and lendeth;
And his seed is blessed.

27 סDepart from evil, and do good;
And dwell for evermore.

28 For the Lord loveth justice,
And forsaketh not His saints;
They are preserved for ever;
But the seed of the wicked shall be cut off.

29 The righteous shall inherit the land,
And dwell therein for ever.

30 פThe mouth of the righteous uttereth wisdom,
And his tongue speaketh justice.

31 עThe law of his God is in his heart;
None of his steps slide.

32 צThe wicked watcheth the righteous,
And seeketh to slay him.

[33]The Lord will not leave him in his hand,
Nor suffer him to be condemned when he is judged.
[34] קWait for the Lord, and keep His way,
And He will exalt thee to inherit the land;
When the wicked are cut off, thou shalt see it.
[35]רI have seen the wicked in great power,
And spreading himself like a leafy tree in its native soil.
[36]But one passed by, and, lo, he was not;
Yea, I sought him, but he could not be found.
[37]שMark the man of integrity, and behold the upright;
For there is a future for the man of peace.
[38]But transgressors shall be destroyed together;
The future of the wicked shall be cut off.
[39]תBut the salvation of the righteous is of the Lord;
He is their stronghold in the time of trouble.
[40]And the Lord helpeth them, and delivereth them;
He delivereth them from the wicked, and saveth them,
Because they have taken refuge in Him.

38A Psalm of David, to make memorial.

[2]O Lord, rebuke me not in Thine anger;
Neither chasten me in Thy wrath.
[3]For Thine arrows are gone deep into me,
And Thy hand is come down upon me.
[4]There is no soundness in my flesh because of Thine indignation;
Neither is there any health in my bones because of my sin.
[5]For mine iniquities are gone over my head;
As a heavy burden they are too heavy for me.
[6]My wounds are noisome, they fester,
Because of my foolishness.
[7]I am bent and bowed down greatly;
I go mourning all the day.
[8]For my loins are filled with burning;
And there is no soundness in my flesh.
[9]I am benumbed and sore crushed;
I groan by reason of the moaning of my heart.
[10]Lord, all my desire is before Thee;
And my sighing is not hid from Thee.
[11]My heart fluttereth, my strength faileth me;
As for the light of mine eyes, it also is gone from me.
[12]My friends and my companions stand aloof from my plague;
And my kinsmen stand afar off.
[13]They also that seek after my life lay snares for me;

And they that seek my hurt speak crafty devices,
And utter deceits all the day.
¹⁴But I am as a deaf man, I hear not;
And I am as a dumb man that openeth not his mouth.
¹⁵Yea, I am become as a man that heareth not,
And in whose mouth are no arguments.
¹⁶For in Thee, O Lord, do I hope;
Thou wilt answer, O Lord my God.
¹⁷For I said: 'Lest they rejoice over me;
When my foot slippeth, they magnify themselves against me.'
¹⁸For I am ready to halt,
And my pain is continually before me.
¹⁹For I do declare mine iniquity;
I am full of care because of my sin.
²⁰But mine enemies are strong in health;
And they that hate me wrongfully are multiplied. ²¹They also that repay evil for good
Are adversaries unto me, because I follow the thing that is good.
²²Forsake me not, O Lord;
O my God, be not far from me.
²³Make haste to help me,
O Lord, my salvation.

39For the Leader, for Jeduthun. A Psalm of David.

²I said: 'I will take heed to my ways,
That I sin not with my tongue;
I will keep a curb upon my mouth,
While the wicked is before me.'
³I was dumb with silence; I held my peace, had no comfort;
And my pain was held in check.
⁴My heart waxed hot within me;
While I was musing, the fire kindled;
Then spoke I with my tongue:
⁵'Lord, make me to know mine end,
And the measure of my days, what it is;
Let me know how short-lived I am.
⁶Behold, Thou hast made my days as hand-breadths;
And mine age is as nothing before Thee;
Surely every man at his best estate is altogether vanity.Selah
⁷Surely man walketh as a mere semblance;
Surely for vanity they are in turmoil;
He heapeth up riches, and knoweth not who shall gather them.
⁸And now, Lord, what wait I for?
My hope, it is in Thee.

⁹Deliver me from all my transgressions;
Make me not the reproach of the base.
¹⁰I am dumb, I open not my mouth;
Because Thou hast done it.
¹¹Remove Thy stroke from off me;
I am consumed by the blow of Thy hand.
¹²With rebukes dost Thou chasten man for iniquity,
And like a moth Thou makest his beauty to consume away;
Surely every man is vanity.Selah
¹³Hear my prayer, O Lord, and give ear unto my cry;
Keep not silence at my tears;
For I am a stranger with Thee,
A sojourner, as all my fathers were.
¹⁴Look away from me, that I may take comfort,
Before I go hence, and be no more.'
40For the Leader. A Psalm of David.

²I waited patiently for the Lord;
And He inclined unto me, and heard my cry.
³He brought me up also out of the tumultuous pit, out of the miry clay;
And He set my feet upon a rock, He established my goings.
⁴And He hath put a new song in my mouth, even praise unto our God;³⁹
Many shall see, and fear,
And shall trust in the Lord.
⁵Happy is the man that hath made the Lord his trust,
And hath not turned unto the arrogant, nor unto such as fall away treacherously.
⁶Many things hast Thou done, O Lord my God,
Even Thy wonderful works, and Thy thoughts toward us;
There is none to be compared unto Thee!
If I would declare and speak of them,
They are more than can be told.
⁷Sacrifice and meal-offering Thou hast no delight in;
Mine ears hast Thou opened;
Burnt-offering and sin-offering hast Thou not required.
⁸Then said I: 'Lo, I am come
With the roll of a book which is prescribed for me;
⁹I delight to do Thy will, O my God;
Yea, Thy law is in my inmost parts.'
¹⁰I have preached righteousness in the great congregation,
Lo, I did not refrain my lips;
O Lord, Thou knowest.
¹¹I have not hid Thy righteousness within my heart;
I have declared Thy faithfulness and Thy salvation;
I have not concealed Thy mercy and Thy truth from the great congregation.

[12]Thou, O Lord, wilt not withhold Thy compassions from me;
Let Thy mercy and Thy truth continually preserve me.
[13]For innumerable evils have compassed me about,
Mine iniquities have overtaken me, so that I am not able to look up;
They are more than the hairs of my head, and my heart hath failed me.
[14]Be pleased, O Lord, to deliver me;
O Lord, make haste to help me.
[15]Let them be ashamed and abashed together
That seek after my soul to sweep it away;
Let them be turned backward and brought to confusion
That delight in my hurt.
[16]Let them be appalled by reason of their shame
That say unto me: 'Aha, aha.'
[17]Let all those that seek Thee rejoice and be glad in Thee;
Let such as love Thy salvation say continually:
'The Lord be magnified.'
[18]But, as for me, that am poor and needy,
The Lord will account it unto me;
Thou art my help and my deliverer;
O my God, tarry not.

41For the Leader. A Psalm of David.

[2]Happy is he that considereth the poor;
The Lord will deliver him in the day of evil.
[3]The Lord preserve him, and keep him alive, let him be called happy in the land;
And deliver not Thou him unto the greed of his enemies.
[4]The Lord support him upon the bed of illness;
Mayest Thou turn all his lying down in his sickness.
[5]As for me, I said: 'O Lord, be gracious unto me;
Heal my soul; for I have sinned against Thee.'
[6]Mine enemies speak evil of me:
'When shall he die, and his name perish?'
[7]And if one come to see me, he speaketh falsehood;
His heart gathereth iniquity to itself;
When he goeth abroad, he speaketh of it.
[8]All that hate me whisper together against me,
Against me do they devise my hurt:
[9]'An evil thing cleaveth fast unto him;
And now that he lieth, he shall rise up no more.'
[10]Yea, mine own familiar friend, in whom I trusted, who did eat of my bread,
Hath lifted up his heel against me.
[11]But Thou, O Lord, be gracious unto me, and raise me up,
That I may requite them.

¹²By this I know that Thou delightest in me,
That mine enemy doth not triumph over me.
¹³And as for me, Thou upholdest me because of mine integrity,
And settest me before Thy face for ever.
¹⁴Blessed be the Lord, the God of Israel,
From everlasting and to everlasting.
Amen, and Amen.

ספר שני
BOOK II

42For the Leader; Maschil of the sons of Korah.

²As the hart panteth after the water brooks,
So panteth my soul after Thee, O God.
³My soul thirsteth for God, for the living God:
'When shall I come and appear before God?'
⁴My tears have been my food day and night,
While they say unto me all the day: 'Where is Thy God?'
⁵These things I remember, and pour out my soul within me,
How I passed on with the throng, and led them to the house of God,
With the voice of joy and praise, a multitude keeping holyday.
⁶Why art thou cast down, O my soul?
And why moanest thou within me? Hope thou in God; for I shall yet praise Him
For the salvation of His countenance.
⁷O my God, my soul is cast down within me;
Therefore do I remember Thee from the land of Jordan,
And the Hermons, from the hill Mizar.
⁸Deep calleth unto deep at the voice of Thy cataracts;
All Thy waves and Thy billows are gone over me.
⁹By day the Lord will command His lovingkindness,
And in the night His song shall be with me,
Even a prayer unto the God of my life.
¹⁰I will say unto God my Rock: 'Why hast Thou forgotten me?
Why go I mourning under the oppression of the enemy?'
¹¹As with a crushing in my bones, mine adversaries taunt me;
While they say unto me all the day: 'Where is Thy God?'
¹²Why art thou cast down, O my soul?
And why moanest thou within me?
Hope thou in God; for I shall yet praise Him,
The salvation of my countenance, and my God.

43Be Thou my judge, O God, and plead my cause against an ungodly nation;
O deliver me from the deceitful and unjust man.

²For Thou art the God of my strength; why hast Thou cast me off?
Why go I mourning under the oppression of the enemy?
³O send out Thy light and Thy truth; let them lead me;
Let them bring me unto Thy holy mountain, and to Thy dwelling-places;
⁴Then will I go unto the altar of God, unto God, my exceeding joy;
And praise Thee upon the harp, O God, my God.
⁵Why art thou cast down, O my soul?
And why moanest thou within me?
Hope thou in God; for I shall yet praise Him,
The salvation of my countenance, and my God.

44For the Leader; [a Psalm] of the sons of Korah. Maschil.

²O God, we have heard with our ears, our fathers have told us;
A work Thou didst in their days, in the days of old.
³Thou with Thy hand didst drive out the nations, and didst plant them in;
Thou didst break the peoples, and didst spread them abroad.
⁴For not by their own sword did they get the land in possession,
Neither did their own arm save them;
But Thy right hand, and Thine arm, and the light of Thy countenance,
Because Thou wast favourable unto them.
⁵Thou art my King, O God;
Command the salvation of Jacob.
⁶Through Thee do we push down our adversaries;
Through Thy name do we tread them under that rise up against us.
⁷For I trust not in my bow,
Neither can my sword save me.
⁸But Thou hast saved us from our adversaries,
And hast put them to shame that hate us.
⁹In God have we gloried all the day,
And we will give thanks unto Thy name for ever.Selah
¹⁰Yet Thou hast cast off, and brought us to confusion;
And goest not forth with our hosts.
¹¹Thou makest us to turn back from the adversary;
And they that hate us spoil at their will.
¹²Thou hast given us like sheep to be eaten;
And hast scattered us among the nations.
¹³Thou sellest Thy people for small gain,
And hast not set their prices high.
¹⁴Thou makest us a taunt to our neighbours,
A scorn and a derision to them that are round about us.
¹⁵Thou makest us a byword among the nations,
A shaking of the head among the peoples.
¹⁶All the day is my confusion before me,

And the shame of my face hath covered me,
¹⁷For the voice of him that taunteth and blasphemeth;
By reason of the enemy and the revengeful.
¹⁸All this is come upon us; yet have we not forgotten Thee,
Neither have we been false to Thy covenant.
¹⁹Our heart is not turned back,
Neither have our steps declined from Thy path;
²⁰Though Thou hast crushed us into a place of jackals,
And covered us with the shadow of death.
²¹If we had forgotten the name of our God,
Or spread forth our hands to a strange god;
²²Would not God search this out?
For He knoweth the secrets of the heart.
²³Nay, but for Thy sake are we killed all the day;
We are accounted as sheep for the slaughter.
²⁴Awake, why sleepest Thou, O Lord?
Arouse Thyself, cast not off for ever.
²⁵Wherefore hidest Thou Thy face,
And forgettest our affliction and our oppression?
²⁶For our soul is bowed down to the dust;
Our belly cleaveth unto the earth.
²⁷Arise for our help,
And redeem us for Thy mercy's sake.

45For the Leader; upon Shoshannim; [a Psalm] of the sons of Korah. Maschil. A Song of loves.

²My heart overfloweth with a goodly matter;
I say: 'My work is concerning a king';
My tongue is the pen of a ready writer.
³Thou art fairer than the children of men;
Grace is poured upon thy lips;
Therefore God hath blessed thee for ever.
⁴Gird thy sword upon thy thigh, O mighty one,
Thy glory and thy majesty.
⁵And in thy majesty prosper, ride on,
In behalf of truth and meekness and righteousness;
And let thy right hand teach thee tremendous things.
⁶Thine arrows are sharp—
The peoples fall under thee—
[They sink] into the heart of the king's enemies.
⁷Thy throne given of God is for ever and ever;
A sceptre of equity is the sceptre of thy kingdom.
⁸Thou hast loved righteousness, and hated wickedness;
Therefore God, thy God, hath anointed thee

With the oil of gladness above thy fellows.

[9]Myrrh, and aloes, and cassia are all thy garments;
Out of ivory palaces stringed instruments have made thee glad.

[10]Kings' daughters are among thy favourites;
At thy right hand doth stand the queen in gold of Ophir.

[11]Hearken, O daughter, and consider, and incline thine ear;
Forget also thine own people, and thy father's house;

[12]So shall the king desire thy beauty;
For he is thy lord; and do homage unto him.

[13]And, O daughter of Tyre, the richest of the people
Shall entreat thy favour with a gift.'

[14]All glorious is the king's daughter within the palace;
Her raiment is of chequer work inwrought with gold.

[15]She shall be led unto the king on richly woven stuff;
The virgins her companions in her train being brought unto thee.

[16]They shall be led with gladness and rejoicing;
They shall enter into the king's palace.

[17]Instead of thy fathers shall be thy sons,
Whom thou shalt make princes in all the land.

[18]I will make thy name to be remembered in all generations;
Therefore shall the peoples praise thee for ever and ever.

46For the Leader; [a Psalm] of the sons of Korah; upon Alamoth. A Song.

[2]God is our refuge and strength,
A very present help in trouble.

[3]Therefore will we not fear, though the earth do change,
And though the mountains be moved into the heart of the seas;

[4]Though the waters thereof roar and foam,
Though the mountains shake at the swelling thereof.Selah

[5]There is a river, the streams whereof make glad the city of God,
The holiest dwelling-place of the Most High.

[6]God is in the midst of her, she shall not be moved;
God shall help her, at the approach of morning.

[7]Nations were in tumult, kingdoms were moved;
He uttered His voice, the earth melted.

[8]The Lord of hosts is with us;
The God of Jacob is our high tower.Selah

[9]Come, behold the works of the Lord,
Who hath made desolations in the earth.

[10]He maketh wars to cease unto the end of the earth;
He breaketh the bow, and cutteth the spear in sunder;
He burneth the chariots in the fire.

[11]'Let be, and know that I am God;

I will be exalted among the nations, I will be exalted in the earth.'
¹²The Lord of hosts is with us;
The God of Jacob is our high tower.Selah

47For the Leader; a Psalm of the sons of Korah.

²O clap your hands, all ye peoples;
Shout unto God with the voice of triumph.
³For the Lord is most high, awful;
A great King over all the earth.
⁴He subdueth peoples under us,
And nations under our feet.
⁵He chooseth our inheritance for us,
The pride of Jacob whom He loveth. Selah
⁶God is gone up amidst shouting,
The Lord amidst the sound of the horn.
⁷Sing praises to God, sing praises;
Sing praises unto our King, sing praises.
⁸For God is the King of all the earth;
Sing ye praises in a skilful song.
⁹God reigneth over the nations;
God sitteth upon His holy throne.
¹⁰The princes of the peoples are gathered together,
The people of the God of Abraham;
For unto God belong the shields of the earth;
He is greatly exalted.

48A Song; a Psalm of the sons of Korah.

²Great is the Lord, and highly to be praised,
In the city of our God, His holy mountain,
³Fair in situation, the joy of the whole earth;
Even mount Zion, the uttermost parts of the north,
The city of the great King.
⁴God in her palaces
Hath made Himself known for a stronghold.
⁵For, lo, the kings assembled themselves,
They came onward together.
⁶They saw, straightway they were amazed;
They were affrighted, they hasted away.
⁷Trembling took hold of them there,
Pangs, as of a woman in travail.
⁸With the east wind
Thou breakest the ships of Tarshish.

⁹As we have heard, so have we seen
In the city of the Lord of hosts, in the city of our God—
God establish it for ever.Selah
¹⁰We have thought on Thy lovingkindness, O God,
In the midst of Thy temple.
¹¹As is Thy name, O God,
So is Thy praise unto the ends of the earth;
Thy right hand is full of righteousness.
¹²Let mount Zion be glad,
Let the daughters of Judah rejoice,
Because of Thy judgments.
¹³Walk about Zion, and go round about her;
Count the towers thereof.
¹⁴Mark ye well her ramparts,
Traverse her palaces;
That ye may tell it to the generation following.
¹⁵For such is God, our God, for ever and ever;
He will guide us eternally.

49For the Leader; a Psalm of the sons of Korah.

²Hear this, all ye peoples;
Give ear, all ye inhabitants of the world,
³Both low and high,
Rich and poor together.
⁴My mouth shall speak wisdom,
And the meditation of my heart shall be understanding.
⁵I will incline mine ear to a parable;
I will open my dark saying upon the harp.
⁶Wherefore should I fear in the days of evil,
When the iniquity of my supplanters compasseth me about,
⁷Of them that trust in their wealth,
And boast themselves in the multitude of their riches?
⁸No man can by any means redeem his brother,
Nor give to God a ransom for him—
⁹For too costly is the redemption of their soul,
And must be let alone for ever—
¹⁰That he should still live alway,
That he should not see the pit.
¹¹For he seeth that wise men die,
The fool and the brutish together perish,
And leave their wealth to others.
¹²Their inward thought is, that their houses shall continue for ever,
And their dwelling-places to all generations;

They call their lands after their own names.
¹³But man abideth not in honour;
He is like the beasts that perish.
¹⁴This is the way of them that are foolish,
And of those who after them approve their sayings. Selah
¹⁵Like sheep they are appointed for the nether-world;
Death shall be their shepherd;
And the upright shall have dominion over them in the morning;
And their form shall be for the nether-world to wear away,
That there be no habitation for it.
¹⁶But God will redeem my soul from the power of the nether-world;
For He shall receive me.Selah
¹⁷Be not thou afraid when one waxeth rich,
When the wealth of his house is increased;
¹⁸For when he dieth he shall carry nothing away;
His wealth shall not descend after him.
¹⁹Though while he lived he blessed his soul:
'Men will praise thee, when thou shalt do well to thyself';
²⁰It shall go to the generation of his fathers;
They shall never see the light.
²¹Man that is in honour understandeth not;
He is like the beasts that perish.

50A Psalm of Asaph.

God, God, the Lord, hath spoken, and called the earth
From the rising of the sun unto the going down thereof.
²Out of Zion, the perfection of beauty,
God hath shined forth.
³Our God cometh, and doth not keep silence;
A fire devoureth before Him,
And round about Him it stormeth mightily.
⁴He calleth to the heavens above,
And to the earth, that He may judge His people:
⁵'Gather My saints together unto Me;
Those that have made a covenant with Me by sacrifice.'
⁶And the heavens declare His righteousness;
For God, He is judge. Selah
⁷'Hear, O My people, and I will speak;
O Israel, and I will testify against thee:
God, thy God, am I.
⁸I will not reprove thee for thy sacrifices;
And thy burnt-offerings are continually before Me.
⁹I will take no bullock out of thy house,

Nor he-goats out of thy folds.
¹⁰For every beast of the forest is Mine,
And the cattle upon a thousand hills.
¹¹I know all the fowls of the mountains;
And the wild beasts of the field are Mine.
¹²If I were hungry, I would not tell thee;
For the world is Mine, and the fulness thereof.
¹³Do I eat the flesh of bulls,
Or drink the blood of goats?
¹⁴Offer unto God the sacrifice of thanksgiving;
And pay thy vows unto the Most High;
¹⁵And call upon Me in the day of trouble;
I will deliver thee, and thou shalt honour Me.'
¹⁶But unto the wicked God saith:
'What hast thou to do to declare My statutes,
And that thou hast taken My covenant in thy mouth?
¹⁷Seeing thou hatest instruction,
And castest My words behind thee.
¹⁸When thou sawest a thief, thou hadst company with him,
And with adulterers was thy portion.
¹⁹Thou hast let loose thy mouth for evil,
And thy tongue frameth deceit. ²⁰Thou sittest and speakest against thy brother;
Thou slanderest thine own mother's son.
²¹These things hast thou done, and should I have kept silence?
Thou hadst thought that I was altogether such a one as thyself;
But I will reprove thee, and set the cause before thine eyes.
²²Now consider this, ye that forget God,
Lest I tear in pieces, and there be none to deliver.
²³Whoso offereth the sacrifice of thanksgiving honoureth Me;
And to him that ordereth his way aright
Will I show the salvation of God.'

51For the Leader. A Psalm of David; ²when Nathan the prophet came unto him, after he had gone in to Bath-sheba.

³Be gracious unto me, O God, according to Thy mercy;
According to the multitude of Thy compassions blot out my transgressions.
⁴Wash me thoroughly from mine iniquity,
And cleanse me from my sin.
⁵For I know my transgressions;
And my sin is ever before me.
⁶Against Thee, Thee only, have I sinned,
And done that which is evil in Thy sight;
That Thou mayest be justified when Thou speakest,

And be in the right when Thou judgest.
⁷Behold, I was brought forth in iniquity,
And in sin did my mother conceive me.
⁸Behold, Thou desirest truth in the inward parts;
Make me, therefore, to know wisdom in mine inmost heart.
⁹Purge me with hyssop, and I shall be clean;
Wash me, and I shall be whiter than snow.
¹⁰Make me to hear joy and gladness;
That the bones which Thou hast crushed may rejoice.
¹¹Hide Thy face from my sins,
Aand blot out all mine iniquities.
¹²Create me a clean heart, O God;
And renew a stedfast spirit within me.
¹³Cast me not away from Thy presence;
And take not Thy holy spirit from me.
¹⁴Restore unto me the joy of Thy salvation;
And let a willing spirit uphold me.
¹⁵Then will I teach transgressors Thy ways;
And sinners shall return unto Thee.
¹⁶Deliver me from bloodguiltiness, O God, Thou God of my salvation;
So shall my tongue sing aloud of Thy righteousness.
¹⁷O Lord, open Thou my lips;
And my mouth shall declare Thy praise.
¹⁸For Thou delightest not in sacrifice, else would I give it;
Thou hast no pleasure in burnt-offering.
¹⁹The sacrifices of God are a broken spirit;
A broken and a contrite heart, O God, Thou wilt not despise.
²⁰Do good in Thy favour unto Zion;
Build Thou the walls of Jerusalem.
²¹Then wilt Thou delight in the sacrifices of righteousness, in burnt-offering and whole offering;
Then will they offer bullocks upon Thine altar.

52For the Leader. Maschil of David; ²when Doeg the Edomite came and told Saul, and said unto him: 'David is come to the house of Ahimelech.'

³Why boastest thou thyself of evil, O mighty man?
The mercy of God endureth continually.
⁴Thy tongue deviseth destruction;
Like a sharp razor, working deceitfully.
⁵Thou lovest evil more than good;
Falsehood rather than speaking righteousness.Selah
⁶Thou lovest all devouring words,
The deceitful tongue.
⁷God will likewise break thee for ever,

He will take thee up, and pluck thee out of thy tent,

And root thee out of the land of the living.Selah

[8]The righteous also shall see, and fear,

And shall laugh at him:

[9]'Lo, this is the man that made not God his stronghold;

But trusted in the abundance of his riches,

And strengthened himself in his wickedness.'

[10]But as for me, I am like a leafy olive-tree in the house of God;

I trust in the mercy of God for ever and ever.

[11]I will give Thee thanks for ever, because Thou hast done it;

And I will wait for Thy name, for it is good, in the presence of Thy saints.

53For the Leader; upon Mahalath. Maschil of David.

[2]The fool hath said in his heart: 'There is no God';

They have dealt corruptly, and have done abominable iniquity; :There is none that doeth good.

[3]God looked forth from heaven upon the children of men,

To see if there were any man of understanding, that did seek after God.

[4]Every one of them is unclean, they are together become impure;

There is none that doeth good, no, not one.

[5]'Shall not the workers of iniquity know it,

Who eat up My people as they eat bread,

And call not upon God?'

[6]There are they in great fear, where no fear was;

For God hath scattered the bones of him that encampeth against thee;

Thou hast put them to shame, because God hath rejected them.

[7]Oh that the salvation of Israel were come out of Zion!

When God turneth the captivity of His people,

Let Jacob rejoice, let Israel be glad.

54For the Leader; with string-music. Maschil of David: [2]when the Ziphites came and said to Saul: 'Doth not David hide himself with us?'

[3]O God, save me by Thy name,

And right me by Thy might.

[4]O God, hear my prayer; give ear to the words of my mouth.

[5]For strangers are risen up against me,

And violent men have sought after my soul;

They have not set God before them.Selah

[6]Behold, God is my helper;

The Lord is for me as the upholder of my soul.

[7]He will requite the evil unto them that lie in wait for me;

Destroy Thou them in Thy truth.

[8]With a freewill-offering will I sacrifice unto Thee;

I will give thanks unto Thy name, O Lord, for it is good.
[9]For He hath delivered me out of all trouble;
And mine eye hath gazed upon mine enemies.

55For the Leader; with string-music. Maschil of David

[2]Give ear, O God, to my prayer;
And hide not Thyself from my supplication.
[3]Attend unto me, and answer me;
I am distraught in my complaint, and will moan;
[4]Because of the voice of the enemy,
Because of the oppression of the wicked;
For they cast mischief upon me,
And in anger they persecute me.
[5]My heart doth writhe within me;
And the terrors of death are fallen upon me.
[6]Fear and trembling come upon me,
And horror hath overwhelmed me.
[7]And I said: 'Oh that I had wings like a dove!
Then would I fly away, and be at rest.
[8]Lo, then would I wander far off,
I would lodge in the wilderness.Selah
[9]I would haste me to a shelter
From the stormy wind and tempest.'
[10]Destroy, O Lord, and divide their tongue;
For I have seen violence and strife in the city.
[11]Day and night they go about it upon the walls thereof;
Iniquity also and mischief are in the midst of it.
[12]Wickedness is in the midst thereof;
Oppression and guile depart not from her broad place.
[13]For it was not an enemy that taunted me,
Then I could have borne it;
Neither was it mine adversary that did magnify himself against me,
Then I would have hid myself from him.
[14]But it was thou, a man mine equal,
My companion, and my familiar friend;
[15]We took sweet counsel together,
In the house of God we walked with the throng.
[16]May He incite death against them,
Let them go down alive into the nether-world;
For evil is in their dwelling, and within them.
[17]As for me, I will call upon God;
And the Lord shall save me.
[18]Evening, and morning, and at noon, will I complain, and moan;

And He hath heard my voice.
¹⁹He hath redeemed my soul in peace so that none came nigh me;
For they were many that strove with me.
²⁰God shall hear, and humble them,
Even He that is enthroned of old,Selah
Such as have no changes,
And fear not God.
²¹He hath put forth his hands against them that were at peace with him;
He hath profaned his covenant.
²²Smoother than cream were the speeches of his mouth,
But his heart was war;
His words were softer than oil,
Yet were they keen-edged swords.
²³Cast thy burden upon the Lord, and He will sustain thee;
He will never suffer the righteous to be moved.
²⁴But Thou, O God, wilt bring them down into the nethermost pit;
Men of blood and deceit shall not live out half their days;
But as for me, I will trust in Thee.

56For the Leader; upon Jonathelem-rehokim. [A Psalm] of David; Michtam; when the Philistines took him in Gath.

²Be gracious unto me, O God, for man would swallow me up;
All the day he fighting oppresseth me.
³They that lie in wait for me would swallow me up all the day;
For they are many that fight against me, O Most High,
⁴In the day that I am afraid,
I will put my trust in Thee.
⁵In God—I will praise His word—
In God do I trust, I will not be afraid;
What can flesh do unto me?
⁶All the day they trouble mine affairs;
All their thoughts are against me for evil.
⁷They gather themselves together, they hide themselves,
They mark my steps;
According as they have waited for my soul.
⁸Because of iniquity cast them out;
In anger bring down the peoples, O God.
⁹Thou has counted my wanderings;
Put Thou my tears into Thy bottle;
Are they not in Thy book?
¹⁰Then shall mine enemies turn back in the day that I call;
This I know, that God is for me.
¹¹In God—I will praise His word—

In the Lord—I will praise His word—
¹²In God do I trust, I will not be afraid;
What can man do unto me?
¹³Thy vows are upon me, O God;
I will render thank-offerings unto Thee.
¹⁴For thou hast delivered my soul from death;
Hast Thou not delivered my feet from stumbling?
That I may walk before God in the light of the living?

57For the Leader; Al-tashheth. [A Psalm] of David; Michtam; when he fled from Saul, in the cave.

²Be gracious unto me, O God, be gracious unto me,
For in Thee hath my soul taken refuge;
Yea, in the shadow of Thy wings will I take refuge,
Until calamities be overpast.
³I will cry unto God Most high;
Unto God that accomplisheth it for me.
⁴He will send from heaven, and save me,
When he that would swallow me up taunteth,Selah
God shall send forth His mercy and His truth.
⁵My soul is among lions, I do lie down among them that are aflame;
Even the sons of men, whose teeth are spears and arrows,
And their tongue a sharp sword.
⁶Be Thou exalted, O God, above the heavens; Thy glory be above all the earth.
⁷They have prepared a net for my steps,
My soul is bowed down;
They have digged a pit before me,
They are fallen into the midst thereof themselves.Selah
⁸My heart is stedfast, O God, my heart is stedfast;
I will sing, yea, I will sing praises.
⁹Awake, my glory; awake, psaltery and harp;
I will awake the dawn.
¹⁰I will give thanks unto Thee, O Lord, among the peoples;
I will sing praises unto Thee among the nations.
¹¹For Thy mercy is great unto the heavens,
And Thy truth unto the skies.
¹²Be Thou exalted, O God, above the heavens;
Thy glory be above all the earth.

58For the Leader; Al-tashheth. [A Psalm] of David; Michtam.

²Do ye indeed speak as a righteous company?
Do ye judge with equity the sons of men?

³Yea, in heart ye work wickedness;
Ye weigh out in the earth the violence of your hands.
⁴The wicked are estranged from the womb;
The speakers of lies go astray as soon as they are born.
⁵Their venom is like the venom of a serpent;
They are like the deaf asp that stoppeth her ear;
⁶Which hearkeneth not to the voice of charmers,
Or of the most cunning binder of spells.
⁷Break their teeth, O God, in their mouth;
Break out the cheek-teeth of the young lions, O Lord.
⁸Let them melt away as water that runneth apace;
When he aimeth his arrows, let them be as though they were cut off.
⁹Let them be as a snail which melteth and passeth away;
Like the untimely births of a woman, that have not seen the sun.
¹⁰Before your pots can feel the thorns,
He will sweep it away with a whirlwind, the raw and the burning alike.
¹¹The righteous shall rejoice when he seeth the vengeance;
He shall wash his feet in the blood of the wicked.
¹²And men shall say: 'Verily there is a reward for the righteous;
Verily there is a God that judgeth in the earth.'

59For the Leader; Al-tashheth. [A Psalm] of David; Michtam; when Saul sent, and they watched the house to kill him.

²Deliver me from mine enemies, O my God;
Set me on high from them that rise up against me.
³Deliver me from the workers of iniquity,
And save me from the men of blood.
⁴For, lo, they lie in wait for my soul;
The impudent gather themselves together against me;
Not for my transgression, nor for my sin, O Lord.
⁵Without my fault, they run and prepare themselves;
Awake Thou to help me, and behold.
⁶Thou therefore, O Lord God of hosts, the God of Israel,
Arouse Thyself to punish all the nations;
Show no mercy to any iniquitous traitors.Selah
⁷They return at evening, they howl like a dog,
And go round about the city.
⁸Behold, they belch out with their mouth;
Swords are in their lips:
'For who doth hear?'
⁹But Thou, O Lord, shalt laugh at them;
Thou shalt have all the nations in derision.
¹⁰Because of his strength, I will wait for Thee;

For God is my high tower.
¹¹The God of my mercy will come to meet me;
God will let me gaze upon mine adversaries.
¹²Slay them not, lest my people forget,
Make them wander to and fro by Thy power, and bring them down,
O Lord our shield.
¹³For the sin of their mouth, and the words of their lips,
Let them even be taken in their pride,
And for cursing and lying which they speak.
¹⁴Consume them in wrath, consume them, that they be no more;
And let them know that God ruleth in Jacob,
Unto the ends of the earth. Selah
¹⁵And they return at evening, they howl like a dog,
And go round about the city;
¹⁶They wander up and down to devour,
And tarry all night if they have not their fill.
¹⁷But as for me, I will sing of Thy strength;
Yea, I will sing aloud of Thy mercy in the morning;
For Thou hast been my high tower,
And a refuge in the day of my distress.
¹⁸O my strength, unto Thee will I sing praises;
For God is my high tower, the God of my mercy.

60For the Leader; upon Shushan Eduth; Michtam of David, to teach; ²when he strove with Aram-naharaim and with Aram-zobah, and Joab returned, and smote of Edom in the Valley of Salt twelve thousand.

³O God, Thou hast cast us off, Thou hast broken us down;
Thou hast been angry; O restore us.
⁴Thou hast made the land to shake, Thou hast cleft it;
Heal the breaches thereof; for it tottereth.
⁵Thou hast made Thy people to see hard things;
Thou hast made us to drink the wine of staggering.
⁶Thou hast given a banner to them that fear Thee,
That it may be displayed because of the truth. Selah
⁷That Thy beloved may be delivered,
Save with Thy right hand, and answer me.
⁸God spoke in His holiness, that I would exult;
That I would divide Shechem, and mete out the valley of Succoth.
⁹Gilead is mine, and Manasseh is mine;
Ephraim also is the defence of my head;
Judah is my sceptre.
¹⁰Moab is my washpot;
Upon Edom do I cast my shoe;

Philistia, cry aloud because of me!
¹¹Who will bring me into the fortified city?
Who will lead me unto Edom?
¹²Hast not Thou, O God, cast us off?
And Thou goest not forth, O God, with our hosts.
¹³Give us help against the adversary;
For vain is the help of man.
¹⁴Through God we shall do valiantly;
For He it is that will tread down our adversaries.

61For the Leader; with string-music. [A Psalm] of David.

²Hear my cry, O God;
Attend unto my prayer.
³From the end of the earth will I call unto Thee, when my heart fainteth;
Lead me to a rock that is too high for me.
⁴For Thou hast been a refuge for me,
A tower of strength in the face of the enemy.
⁵I will dwell in Thy Tent for ever;
I will take refuge in the covert of Thy wings.Selah
⁶For Thou, O God, hast heard my vows;
Thou hast granted the heritage of those that fear Thy name.
⁷Mayest Thou add days unto the king's days!
May his years be as many generations!
⁸May he be enthroned before God for ever!
Appoint mercy and truth, that they may preserve him.
⁹So will I sing praise unto Thy name for ever,
That I may daily perform my vows.

62For the Leader; for Jeduthun. A Psalm of David.

²Only for God doth my soul wait in stillness;
From Him cometh my salvation.
³He only is my rock and my salvation,
My high tower, I shall not be greatly moved.
⁴How long will ye set upon a man,
That ye may slay him, all of you,
As a leaning wall, a tottering fence?
⁵They only devise to thrust him down from his height, delighting in lies;
They bless with their mouth, but they curse inwardly.Selah
⁶Only for God wait thou in stillness, my soul;
For from Him cometh my hope.
⁷He only is my rock and my salvation,
My high tower, I shall not be moved.

[8]Upon God resteth my salvation and my glory;
The rock of my strength, and my refuge, is in God.
[9]Trust in Him at all times, ye people;
Pour out your heart before Him;
God is a refuge for us.Selah
[10]Men of low degree are vanity, and men of high degree are a lie;
If they be laid in the balances, they are together lighter than vanity.
[11]Trust not in oppression,
And put not vain hope in robbery;
If riches increase, set not your heart thereon.
[12]God hath spoken once,
Twice have I heard this:
That strength belongeth unto God;
[13]Also unto Thee, O Lord, belongeth mercy;
For Thou renderest to every man according to his work.

63A Psalm of David, when he was in the wilderness of Judah.

[2]O God, Thou art my God, earnestly will I seek Thee;
My soul thirsteth for Thee, my flesh longeth for Thee,
In a dry and weary land, where no water is.
[3]So have I looked for Thee in the sanctuary,
To see Thy power and Thy glory.
[4]For Thy lovingkindness is better than life;
My lips shall praise Thee.
[5]So will I bless Thee as long as I live;
In Thy name will I lift up my hands.
[6]My soul is satisfied as with marrow and fatness;
And my mouth doth praise Thee with joyful lips;
[7]When I remember Thee upon my couch,
And meditate on Thee in the nightwatches.
[8]For Thou hast been my help,
And in the shadow of Thy wings do I rejoice.
[9]My soul cleaveth unto Thee;
Thy right hand holdeth me fast.
[10]But those that seek my soul, to destroy it,
Shall go into the nethermost parts of the earth.
[11]They shall be hurled to the power of the sword;
They shall be a portion for foxes.
[12]But the king shall rejoice in God;
Every one that sweareth by Him shall glory;
For the mouth of them that speak lies shall be stopped.

64For the Leader. A Psalm of David.

[2]Hear my voice, O God, in my complaint;
Preserve my life from the terror of the enemy.
[3]Hide me from the council of evil-doers;
From the tumult of the workers of iniquity;
[4]Who have whet their tongue like a sword,
And have aimed their arrow, a poisoned word;
[5]That they may shoot in secret places at the blameless;
Suddenly do they shoot at him, and fear not.
[6]They encourage one another in an evil matter;
They converse of laying snares secretly;
They ask, who would see them.
[7]They search out iniquities, they have accomplished a diligent search;
Even in the inward thought of every one, and the deep heart.
[8]But God doth shoot at them with an arrow suddenly;
Thence are their wounds.
[9]So they make their own tongue a stumbling unto themselves;
All that see them shake the head.
[10]And all men fear;
And they declare the work of God,
And understand His doing.
[11]The righteous shall be glad in the Lord, and shall take refuge in Him;
And all the upright in heart shall glory.

65For the Leader. A Psalm. A Song of David.

[2]Praise waiteth for Thee, O God, in Zion;
And unto Thee the vow is performed.
[3]O Thou that hearest prayer,
Unto Thee doth all flesh come.
[4]The tale of iniquities is too heavy for me;
As for our transgressions, Thou wilt pardon them.
[5]Happy is the man whom Thou choosest, and bringest near,
That he may dwell in Thy courts;
May we be satisfied with the goodness of Thy house,
The holy place of Thy temple!
[6]With wondrous works dost Thou answer us in righteousness,
O God of our salvation;
Thou the confidence of all the ends of the earth,
And of the far distant seas;
[7]Who by Thy strength settest fast the mountains,
Who art girded about with might;
[8]Who stillest the roaring of the seas, the roaring of their waves,
And the tumult of the peoples;

⁹So that they that dwell in the uttermost parts stand in awe of Thy signs;
Thou makest the outgoings of the morning and evening to rejoice.
¹⁰Thou hast remembered the earth, and watered her, greatly enriching her,
With the river of God that is full of water;
Thou preparest them corn, for so preparest Thou her.
¹¹Watering her ridges abundantly,
Settling down the furrows thereof,
Thou makest her soft with showers;
Thou blessest the growth thereof.
¹²Thou crownest the year with Thy goodness;
And Thy paths drop fatness.
¹³The pastures of the wilderness do drop;
And the hills are girded with joy.
¹⁴The meadows are clothed with flocks;
The valleys also are covered over with corn;
They shout for joy, yea, they sing.

66For the Leader. A Song, a Psalm.

Shout unto God, all the earth;
²Sing praises unto the glory of His name;
Make His praise glorious.
³Say unto God: 'How tremendous is Thy work!
Through the greatness of Thy power shall Thine enemies dwindle away before Thee.
⁴All the earth shall worship Thee,
And shall sing praises unto Thee;
They shall sing praises to Thy name.'Selah
⁵Come, and see the works of God;
He is terrible in His doing toward the children of men.
⁶He turned the sea into dry land;
They went through the river on foot;
There let us rejoice in Him!
⁷Who ruleth by His might for ever;
His eyes keep watch upon the nations;
Let not the rebellious exalt themselves.Selah
⁸Bless our God, ye peoples,
And make the voice of His praise to be heard;
⁹Who hath set our soul in life,
And suffered not our foot to be moved,
¹⁰For Thou, O God, hast tried us;
Thou hast refined us, as silver is refined.
¹¹Thou didst bring us into the hold;
Thou didst lay constraint upon our loins.
¹²Thou hast caused men to ride over our heads;

We went through fire and through water;
But Thou didst bring us out unto abundance.
¹³I will come into Thy house with burnt-offerings,
I will perform unto Thee my vows,
¹⁴Which my lips have uttered,
And my mouth hath spoken, when I was in distress.
¹⁵I will offer unto Thee burnt-offerings of fatlings,
With the sweet smoke of rams;
I will offer bullocks with goats.Selah
¹⁶Come, and hearken, all ye that fear God,
And I will declare what He hath done for my soul.
¹⁷I cried unto Him with my mouth,
And He was extolled with my tongue.
¹⁸If I had regarded iniquity in my heart,
The Lord would not hear;
¹⁹But verily God hath heard;
He hath attended to the voice of my prayer.
²⁰Blessed be God,
Who hath not turned away my prayer, nor His mercy from me.

67For the Leader; with string-music. A Psalm, a Song.

²God be gracious unto us, and bless us;
May He cause His face to shine toward us;Selah
³That Thy way may be known upon earth,
Thy salvation among all nations.
⁴Let the peoples give thanks unto Thee, O God;
Let the peoples give thanks unto Thee, all of them.
⁵O let the nations be glad and sing for joy;
For Thou wilt judge the peoples with equity,
And lead the nations upon earth.Selah
⁶Let the peoples give thanks unto Thee, O God;
Let the peoples give thanks unto Thee, all of them.
⁷The earth hath yielded her increase;
May God, our own God, bless us.
⁸May God bless us;
And let all the ends of the earth fear Him.

68For the Leader. A Psalm of David, a Song.

²Let God arise, let His enemies be scattered;
And let them that hate Him flee before Him.
³As smoke is driven away, so drive them away;
As wax melteth before the fire,

So let the wicked perish at the presence of God.
⁴But let the righteous be glad, let them exult before God;
Yea, let them rejoice with gladness.
⁵Sing unto God, sing praises to His name;
Extol Him that rideth upon the skies, whose name is the Lord;
And exult ye before Him.
⁶A father of the fatherless, and a judge of the widows,
Is God in His holy habitation.
⁷God maketh the solitary to dwell in a house;
He bringeth out the prisoners into prosperity;
The rebellious dwell but in a parched land.
⁸O God, when Thou wentest forth before Thy people,
When Thou didst march through the wilderness; Selah
⁹The earth trembled, the heavens also dropped at the presence of God;
Even yon Sinai trembled at the presence of God, the God of Israel.
¹⁰A bounteous rain didst Thou pour down, O God;
When Thine inheritance was weary, Thou didst confirm it.
¹¹Thy flock settled therein;
Thou didst prepare in Thy goodness for the poor, O God.
¹²The Lord giveth the word;
The women that proclaim the tidings are a great host.
¹³Kings of armies flee, they flee;
And she that tarrieth at home divideth the spoil.
¹⁴When ye lie among the sheepfolds,
The wings of the dove are covered with silver,
And her pinions with the shimmer of gold. ¹⁵When the Almighty scattereth kings therein,
It snoweth in Zalmon.
¹⁶A mountain of God is the mountain of Bashan;
A mountain of peaks is the mountain of Bashan.
¹⁷Why look ye askance, ye mountains of peaks,
At the mountain which God hath desired for His abode?
Yea, the Lord will dwell therein for ever.
¹⁸The chariots of God are myriads, even thousands upon thousands;
The Lord is among them, as in Sinai, in holiness.
¹⁹Thou hast ascended on high, Thou hast led captivity captive;
Thou hast received gifts among men,
Yea, among the rebellious also, that the Lord God might dwell there.
²⁰Blessed be the Lord, day by day He beareth our burden,
Even the God who is our salvation.Selah
²¹God is unto us a God of deliverances;
And unto God the Lord belong the issues of death.
²²Surely God will smite through the head of His enemies,
The hairy scalp of him that goeth about in his guiltiness.
²³The Lord said: 'I will bring back from Bashan,

I will bring them back from the depths of the sea;
²⁴That thy foot may wade through blood,
That the tongue of thy dogs may have its portion from thine enemies.'
²⁵They see Thy goings, O God,
Even the goings of my God, my King, in holiness.
²⁶The singers go before, the minstrels follow after,
In the midst of damsels playing upon timbrels.
²⁷'Bless ye God in full assemblies,
Even the Lord, ye that are from the fountain of Israel.'
²⁸There is Benjamin, the youngest, ruling them,
The princes of Judah their council,
The princes of Zebulun, the princes of Naphtali.
²⁹Thy God hath commanded thy strength;
Be strong, O God, Thou that hast wrought for us
³⁰Out of Thy temple at Jerusalem,
Whither kings shall bring presents unto Thee.
³¹Rebuke the wild beast of the reeds,
The multitude of the bulls, with the calves of the peoples,
Every one submitting himself with pieces of silver;
He hath scattered the peoples that delight in war!
³²Nobles shall come out of Egypt;
Ethiopia shall hasten to stretch out her hands unto God.
³³Sing unto God, ye kingdoms of the earth;
O sing praises unto the Lord;Selah
³⁴To Him that rideth upon the heavens of heavens, which are of old;
Lo, He uttereth His voice, a mighty voice.
³⁵Ascribe ye strength unto God;
His majesty is over Israel,
And His strength is in the skies.
³⁶Awful is God out of thy holy places;
The God of Israel, He giveth strength and power unto the people;
Blessed be God.

69For the Leader; upon Shoshannim. [A Psalm] of David.

²Save me, O God;
For the waters are come in even unto the soul.
³I am sunk in deep mire, where there is no standing;
I am come into deep waters, and the flood overwhelmeth me.
⁴I am weary of my crying; my throat is dried;
Mine eyes fail while I wait for my God.
⁵They that hate me without a cause are more than the hairs of my head;
They that would cut me off, being mine enemies wrongfully, are many;
Should I restore that which I took not away?

[6]O God, Thou knowest my folly;
And my trespasses are not hid from Thee.
[7]Let not them that wait for Thee be ashamed through me, O Lord God of hosts;
Let not those that seek Thee be brought to confusion through me, O God of Israel.
[8]Because for Thy sake I have borne reproach;
Confusion hath covered my face.
[9]I am become a stranger unto my brethren,
And an alien unto my mother's children.
[10]Because zeal for Thy house hath eaten me up,
And the reproaches of them that reproach Thee are fallen upon me.
[11]And I wept with my soul with fasting,
And that became unto me a reproach.
[12]I made sackcloth also my garment,
And I became a byword unto them.
[13]They that sit in the gate talk of me;
And I am the song of the drunkards.
[14]But as for me, let my prayer be unto Thee, O Lord, in an acceptable time;
O God, in the abundance of Thy mercy,
Answer me with the truth of Thy salvation.
[15]Deliver me out of the mire, and let me not sink;
Let me be delivered from them that hate me, and out of the deep waters.
[16]Let not the waterflood overwhelm me,
Neither let the deep swallow me up;
And let not the pit shut her mouth upon me.
[17]Answer me, O Lord, for Thy mercy is good;
According to the multitude of Thy compassions turn Thou unto me.
[18]And hide not Thy face from Thy servant;
For I am in distress; answer me speedily.
[19]Draw nigh unto my soul, and redeem it;
Ransom me because of mine enemies.
[20]Thou knowest my reproach, and my shame, and my confusion;
Mine adversaries are all before Thee.
[21]Reproach hath broken my heart; and I am sore sick;
And I looked for some to show compassion, but there was none;
And for comforters, but I found none.
[22]Yea, they put poison into my food;
And in my thirst they gave me vinegar to drink.
[23]Let their table before them become a snare;
And when they are in peace, let it become a trap.
[24]Let their eyes be darkened, that they see not;
And make their loins continually to totter.
[25]Pour out Thine indignation upon them,
And let the fierceness of Thine anger overtake them.
[26]Let their encampment be desolate;

Let none dwell in their tents.
²⁷For they persecute him whom Thou hast smitten;
And they tell of the pain of those whom Thou hast wounded.
²⁸Add iniquity unto their iniquity;
And let them not come into Thy righteousness.
²⁹Let them be blotted out of the book of the living,
And not be written with the righteous.
³⁰But I am afflicted and in pain;
Let Thy salvation, O God, set me up on high.
³¹I will praise the name of God with a song,
And will magnify Him with thanksgiving.
³²And it shall please the Lord better than a bullock
That hath horns and hoofs.
³³The humble shall see it, and be glad;
Ye that seek after God, let your heart revive.
³⁴For the Lord hearkeneth unto the needy,
And despiseth not His prisoners.
³⁵Let heaven and earth praise Him,
The seas, and every thing that moveth therein.
³⁶For God will save Zion, and build the cities of Judah;
And they shall abide there, and have it in possession.
³⁷The seed also of His servants shall inherit it;
And they that love His name shall dwell therein.

70For the Leader. [A Psalm] of David; to make memorial.

²O God, to deliver me,
O Lord, to help me, make haste.
³Let them be ashamed and abashed
That seek after my soul;
Let them be turned backward and brought to confusion
That delight in my hurt.
⁴Let them be turned back by reason of their shame
That say: 'Aha, aha.'
⁵Let all those that seek Thee rejoice and be glad in Thee;
And let such as love Thy salvation say continually:
'Let God be magnified.'
⁶But I am poor and needy,
O God, make haste unto me;
Thou art my help and my deliverer;
O Lord, tarry not.

71In Thee, O Lord, have I taken refuge;
Let me never be ashamed.

²Deliver me in Thy righteousness, and rescue me;
Incline Thine ear unto me, and save me.
³Be Thou to me a sheltering rock, whereunto I may continually resort,
Which Thou hast appointed to save me;
For Thou art my rock and my fortress.
⁴O my God, rescue me out of the hand of the wicked,
Out of the grasp of the unrighteous and ruthless man.
⁵For Thou art my hope;
O Lord God, my trust from my youth.
⁶Upon Thee have I stayed myself from birth;
Thou art he that took me out of my mother's womb;
My praise is continually of Thee.
⁷I am as a wonder unto many;
But Thou art my strong refuge.
⁸My mouth shall be filled with Thy praise,
And with Thy glory all the day.
⁹Cast me not off in the time of old age;
When my strength faileth, forsake me not.
¹⁰For mine enemies speak concerning me,
And they that watch for my soul take counsel together,
¹¹Saying: 'God hath forsaken him;
Pursue and take him; for there is none to deliver.'
¹²O God, be not far from me;
O my God, make haste to help me.
¹³Let them be ashamed and consumed that are adversaries to my soul;
Let them be covered with reproach and confusion that seek my hurt.
¹⁴But as for me, I will hope continually,
And will praise Thee yet more and more.
¹⁵My mouth shall tell of Thy righteousness,
And of Thy salvation all the day;
For I know not the numbers thereof.
¹⁶I will come with Thy mighty acts, O Lord God;
I will make mention of Thy righteousness, even of Thine only.
¹⁷O God, Thou hast taught me from my youth;
And until now do I declare Thy wondrous works.
¹⁸And even unto old age and hoary hairs, O God, forsake me not;
Until I have declared Thy strength unto the next generation,
Thy might to every one that is to come.
¹⁹Thy righteousness also, O God, which reacheth unto high heaven;
Thou who hast done great things,
O God, who is like unto Thee?
²⁰Thou, who hast made me to see many and sore troubles,
Wilt quicken me again, and bring me up again from the depths of the earth.
²¹Thou wilt increase my greatness,

And turn and comfort me.
²²I also will give thanks unto Thee with the psaltery,
Even unto Thy truth, O my God;
I will sing praises unto Thee with the harp,
O Thou Holy One of Israel.
²³My lips shall greatly rejoice when I sing praises unto Thee;
And my soul, which Thou hast redeemed.
²⁴My tongue also shall tell of Thy righteousness all the day;
For they are ashamed, for they are abashed, that seek my hurt.

72[A Psalm] of Solomon.

Give the king Thy judgments, O God,
And Thy righteousness unto the king's son;
²That he may judge Thy people with righteousness,
And Thy poor with justice.
³Let the mountains bear peace to the people,
And the hills, through righteousness.
⁴May he judge the poor of the people,
And save the children of the needy,
And crush the oppressor.
⁵They shall fear Thee while the sun endureth,
And so long as the moon, throughout all generations.
⁶May he come down like rain upon the mown grass,
As showers that water the earth.
⁷In his days let the righteous flourish,
And abundance of peace, till the moon be no more.
⁸May he have dominion also from sea to sea,
And from the River unto the ends of the earth.
⁹Let them that dwell in the wilderness bow before him;
And his enemies lick the dust.
¹⁰The kings of Tarshish and of the isles shall render tribute;
The kings of Sheba and Seba shall offer gifts.
¹¹Yea, all kings shall prostrate themselves before him;
All nations shall serve him.
¹²For he will deliver the needy when he crieth; the poor also, and him that hath no helper.
¹³He will have pity on the poor and needy,
And the souls of the needy he will save.
¹⁴He will redeem their soul from oppression and violence,
And precious will their blood be in his sight.
¹⁵That they may live, and that he may give them of the gold of Sheba,
That they may pray for him continually,
Yea, bless him all the day.
¹⁶May he be as a rich cornfield in the land upon the top of the mountains;

May his fruit rustle like Lebanon;
And may they blossom out of the city like grass of the earth.
¹⁷May his name endure for ever;
May his name be continued as long as the sun;
May men also bless themselves by him;
May all nations call him happy.
¹⁸Blessed be the Lord God, the God of Israel,
Who only doeth wondrous things;
¹⁹And blessed be His glorious name for ever;
And let the whole earth be filled with His glory.
Amen, and Amen.
²⁰The prayers of David the son of Jesse are ended.
ספר שלישי
BOOK III

73A Psalm of Asaph.

Surely God is good to Israel,
Even to such as are pure in heart.
²But as for me, my feet were almost gone;
My steps had well nigh slipped.
³For I was envious at the arrogant,
When I saw the prosperity of the wicked.
⁴For there are no pangs at their death,
And their body is sound.
⁵In the trouble of man they are not;
Neither are they plagued like men.
⁶Therefore pride is as a chain about their neck;
Violence covereth them as a garment.
⁷Their eyes stand forth from fatness;
They are gone beyond the imaginations of their heart.
⁸They scoff, and in wickedness utter oppression;
They speak as if there were none on high.
⁹They have set their mouth against the heavens,
And their tongue walketh through the earth.
¹⁰Therefore His people return hither;
And waters of fullness are drained out by them.
¹¹And they say: 'How doth God know?
And is there knowledge in the Most High?'
¹²Behold, such are the wicked;
And they that are always at ease increase riches.
¹³Surely in vain have I cleansed my heart,
And washed my hands in innocency;
¹⁴For all the day have I been plagued,

And my chastisement came every morning.
¹⁵If I had said: 'I will speak thus',
Behold, I had been faithless to the generation of Thy children.
¹⁶And when I pondered how I might know this,
It was wearisome in mine eyes;
¹⁷Until I entered into the sanctuary of God,
And considered their end.
¹⁸Surely Thou settest them in slippery places;
Thou hurlest them down to utter ruin.
¹⁹How are they become a desolation in a moment!
They are wholly consumed by terrors.
²⁰As a dream when one awaketh,
So, O Lord, when Thou arousest Thyself, Thou wilt despise their semblance.
²¹For my heart was in a ferment,
And I was pricked in my reins.
²²But I was brutish, and ignorant;
I was as a beast before Thee.
²³Nevertheless I am continually with Thee;
Thou holdest my right hand.
²⁴Thou wilt guide me with Thy counsel,
And afterward receive me with glory.
²⁵Whom have I in heaven but Thee?
And beside Thee I desire none upon earth.
²⁶My flesh and my heart faileth;
But God is the rock of my heart and my portion for ever.
²⁷For, lo, they that go far from Thee shall perish;
Thou dost destroy all them that go astray from Thee.
²⁸But as for me, the nearness of God is my good;
I have made the Lord God my refuge,
That I may tell of all Thy works.

74Maschil of Asaph.

Why, O God, hast Thou cast us off for ever?
Why doth Thine anger smoke against the flock of Thy pasture?
²Remember Thy congregation, which Thou hast gotten of old,
Which Thou hast redeemed to be the tribe of Thine inheritance;
And mount Zion, wherein Thou hast dwelt.
³Lift up Thy steps because of the perpetual ruins,
Even all the evil that the enemy hath done in the sanctuary.
⁴Thine adversaries have roared in the midst of Thy meeting-place;
They have set up their own signs for signs.
⁵It seemed as when men wield upwards
Axes in a thicket of trees.

⁶And now all the carved work thereof together
They strike down with hatchet and hammers.
⁷They have set Thy sanctuary on fire;
They have profaned the dwelling-place of Thy name even to the ground.
⁸They said in their heart: 'Let us make havoc of them altogether';
They have burned up all the meeting-places of God in the land.
⁹We see not our signs;
There is no more any prophet;
Neither is there among us any that knoweth how long.
¹⁰How long, O God, shall the adversary reproach?
Shall the enemy blaspheme Thy name for ever?
¹¹Why withdrawest Thou Thy hand, even Thy right hand?
Draw it out of Thy bosom and consume them.
¹²Yet God is my King of old, Working salvation in the midst of the earth.
¹³Thou didst break the sea in pieces by Thy strength;
Thou didst shatter the heads of the sea-monsters in the waters.
¹⁴Thou didst crush the heads of leviathan,
Thou gavest him to be food to the folk inhabiting the wilderness.
¹⁵Thou didst cleave fountain and brook;
Thou driedst up ever-flowing rivers.
¹⁶Thine is the day, Thine also the night;
Thou hast established luminary and sun.
¹⁷Thou hast set all the borders of the earth;
Thou hast made summer and winter.
¹⁸Remember this, how the enemy hath reproached the Lord,
And how a base people have blasphemed Thy name.
¹⁹O deliver not the soul of Thy turtle-dove unto the wild beast;
Forget not the life of Thy poor for ever.
²⁰Look upon the covenant;
For the dark places of the land are full of the habitations of violence.
²¹O let not the oppressed turn back in confusion;
Let the poor and needy praise Thy name.
²²Arise, O God, plead Thine own cause;
Remember Thy reproach all the day at the hand of the base man.
²³Forget not the voice of Thine adversaries,
The tumult of those that rise up against Thee which ascendeth continually.

75For the Leader; Al-tashheth. A Psalm of Asaph, a Song.

²We give thanks unto Thee, O God,
We give thanks, and Thy name is near;
Men tell of Thy wondrous works.
³'When I take the appointed time,
I Myself will judge with equity.

⁴When the earth and all the inhabitants thereof are dissolved,
I Myself establish the pillars of it.'Selah
⁵I say unto the arrogant 'Deal not arrogantly';
And to the wicked 'Lift not up the horn.'
⁶Lift not up your horn on high;
Speak not insolence with a haughty neck.
⁷For neither from the east, nor from the west,
Nor yet from the wilderness, cometh lifting up.
⁸For God is judge;
He putteth down one, and lifteth up another.
⁹For in the hand of the Lord there is a cup, with foaming wine, full of mixture,
And He poureth out of the same;
Surely the dregs thereof, all the wicked of the earth shall drain them, and drink them.
¹⁰But as for me, I will declare for ever,
I will sing praises to the God of Jacob.
¹¹All the horns of the wicked also will I cut off;
But the horns of the righteous shall be lifted up.

76For the Leader; with string-music. A Psalm of Asaph, a Song.

²In Judah is God known;
His name is great in Israel.
³In Salem also is set His tabernacle,
And His dwelling-place in Zion.
⁴There He broke the fiery shafts of the bow;
The shield, and the sword, and the battle.Selah
⁵Glorious art Thou and excellent, coming down from the mountains of prey.
⁶The stout-hearted are bereft of sense, they sleep their sleep;
And none of the men of might have found their hands.
⁷At Thy rebuke, O God of Jacob,
They are cast into a dead sleep, the riders also and the horses.
⁸Thou, even Thou, art terrible;
And who may stand in Thy sight when once Thou art angry?
⁹Thou didst cause sentence to be heard from heaven;
The earth feared, and was still,
¹⁰When God arose to judgment,
To save all the humble of the earth.Selah
¹¹Surely the wrath of man shall praise Thee;
The residue of wrath shalt Thou gird upon Thee.
¹²Vow, and pay unto the Lord your God;
Let all that are round about Him bring presents unto Him that is to be feared;
¹³He minisheth the spirit of princes;
He is terrible to the kings of the earth.

77For the Leader; for Jeduthun. A Psalm of Asaph.

[2]I will lift up my voice unto God, an cry;
I will lift up my voice unto God, that He may give ear unto me.
[3]In the day of my trouble I seek the Lord;
With my hand uplifted, [mine eye] streameth in the night without ceasing;
My soul refuseth to be comforted.
[4]When I think thereon, O God, I must moan;
When I muse thereon, my spirit fainteth.Selah
[5]Thou holdest fast the lids of mine eyes;
I am troubled, and cannot speak.
[6]I have pondered the days of old, the years of ancient times.
[7]In the night I will call to remembrance my song;
I will commune with mine own heart;
And my spirit maketh diligent search
[8]'Will the Lord cast off for ever?
And will He be favourable no more?
[9]Is His mercy clean gone for ever?
Is His promise come to an end for evermore?
[10]Hath God forgotten to be gracious?
Hath He in anger shut up his compassions?'Selah
[11]And I say 'This is my weakness,
That the right hand of the Most High could change.
[12]I will make mention of the deeds of the Lord;
Yea, I will remember Thy wonders of old.
[13]I will meditate also upon all Thy work,
And muse on Thy doings.'
[14]O God, Thy way is in holiness;
Who is a great god like unto God?
[15]Thou art the God that doest wonders;
Thou hast made known Thy strength among the peoples.
[16]Thou hast with Thine arm redeemed Thy people,
The sons of Jacob and Joseph.Selah
[17]The waters saw Thee, O God;
The waters saw Thee, they were in pain;
The depths also trembled.
[18]The clouds flooded forth waters;
The skies sent out a sound;
Thine arrows also went abroad.
[19]The voice of Thy thunder was in the whirlwind;
The lightnings lighted up the world;
The earth trembled and shook.
[20]Thy way was in the sea,
And Thy path in the great waters,

And Thy footsteps were not known.
²¹Thou didst lead Thy people like a flock,
By the hand of Moses and Aaron.

78Maschil of Asaph.

Give ear, O my people, to my teaching;
Incline your ears to the words of my mouth.
²I will open my mouth with a parable;
I will utter dark sayings concerning days of old;
³That which we have heard and known,
And our fathers have told us,
⁴We will not hide from their children,
Telling to the generation to come the praises of the Lord,
And His strength, and His wondrous works that He hath done.
⁵For He established a testimony in Jacob,
And appointed a law in Israel,
Which He commanded our fathers,
That they should make them known to their children;
⁶That the generation to come might know them, even the children that should be born;
Who should arise and tell them to their children,
⁷That they might put their confidence in God,
And not forget the works of God,
But keep His commandments;
⁸And might not be as their fathers,
A stubborn and rebellious generation;
A generation that set not their heart aright,
And whose spirit was not stedfast with God.
⁹The children of Ephraim were as archers handling the bow,
That turned back in the day of battle.
¹⁰They kept not the covenant of God,
And refused to walk in His law;
¹¹And they forgot His doings,
And His wondrous works that He had shown them.
¹²Marvellous things did He in the sight of their fathers,
In the land of Egypt, in the field of Zoan.
¹³He cleaved the sea, and caused them to pass through;
And He made the waters to stand as a heap.
¹⁴By day also He led them with a cloud,
And all the night with a light of fire.
¹⁵He cleaved rocks in the wilderness,
And gave them drink abundantly as out of the great deep.
¹⁶He brought streams also out of the rock,
And caused waters to run down like rivers.

[17]Yet went they on still to sin against Him,
To rebel against the Most High in the desert.
[18]And they tried God in their heart
By asking food for their craving.
[19]Yea, they spoke against God;
They said 'Can God prepare a table in the wilderness?
[20]Behold, He smote the rock, that waters gushed out,
And streams overflowed;
Can He give bread also?
Or will He provide flesh for His people?'
[21]Therefore the Lord heard, and was wroth;
And a fire was kindled against Jacob,
And anger also went up against Israel;
[22]Because they believed not in God,
And trusted not in His salvation.
[23]And He commanded the skies above,
And opened the doors of heaven;
[24]And He caused manna to rain upon them for food,
And gave them of the corn of heaven.
[25]Man did eat the bread of the mighty;
He sent them provisions to the full.
[26]He caused the east wind to set forth in heaven;
And by His power He brought on the south wind.
[27]He caused flesh also to rain upon them as the dust,
And winged fowl as the sand of the seas;
[28]And He let it fall in the midst of their camp,
Round about their dwellings.
[29]So they did eat, and were well filled;
And He gave them that which they craved.
[30]They were not estranged from their craving,
Their food was yet in their mouths,
[31]When the anger of God went up against them,
And slew of the lustieth among them,
And smote down the young men of Israel.
[32]For all this they sinned still,
And believed not in His wondrous works.
[33]Therefore He ended their days as a breath,
And their years in terror.
[34]When He slew them, then they would inquire after Him,
And turn back and seek God earnestly.
[35]And they remembered that God was their Rock,
And the Most High God their redeemer.
[36]But they beguiled Him with their mouth,
And lied unto Him with their tongue.

³⁷For their heart was not stedfast with Him,
Neither were they faithful in His covenant.
³⁸But He, being full of compassion, forgiveth iniquity, and destroyeth not;
Yea, many a time doth He turn His anger away,
And doth not stir up all His wrath.
³⁹So He remembered that they were but flesh,
A wind that passeth away, and cometh not again.
⁴⁰How oft did they rebel against Him in the wilderness,
And grieve Him in the desert!
⁴¹And still again they tried God,
And set bounds to the Holy One of Israel.
⁴²They remembered not His hand,
Nor the day when He redeemed them from the adversary.
⁴³How He set His signs in Egypt,
And His wonders in the field of Zoan;
⁴⁴And turned their rivers into blood,
So that they could not drink their streams.
⁴⁵He sent among them swarms of flies, which devoured them;
And frogs, which destroyed them.
⁴⁶He gave also their increase unto the caterpillar,
And their labour unto the locust.
⁴⁷He destroyed their vines with hail,
And their sycamore-trees with frost.
⁴⁸He gave over their cattle also to the hail,
And their flocks to fiery bolts.
⁴⁹He sent forth upon them the fierceness of His anger,
Wrath, and indignation, and trouble,
A sending of messengers of evil.
⁵⁰He levelled a path for His anger;
He spared not their soul from death,
But gave their life over to the pestilence;
⁵¹And smote all the first-born in Egypt,
The first-fruits of their strength in the tents of Ham;
⁵²But He made His own people to go forth like sheep,
And guided them in the wilderness like a flock.
⁵³And He led them safely, and they feared not;
But the sea overwhelmed their enemies.
⁵⁴And He brought them to His holy border,
To the mountain, which His right hand had gotten.
⁵⁵He drove out the nations also before them,
And allotted them for an inheritance by line,
And made the tribes of Israel to dwell in their tents.
⁵⁶Yet they tried and provoked God, the Most High,
And kept not His testimonies;

⁵⁷But turned back, and dealt treacherously like their fathers;
They were turned aside like a deceitful bow.
⁵⁸For they provoked Him with their high places,
And moved Him to jealousy with their graven images.
⁵⁹God heard, and was wroth,
And He greatly abhorred Israel;
⁶⁰And He forsook the tabernacle of Shiloh,
The tent which He had made to dwell among men;
⁶¹And delivered His strength into captivity,
And His glory into the adversary's hand.
⁶²He gave His people over also unto the sword;
And was wroth with His inheritance.
⁶³Fire devoured their young men;
And their virgins had no marriage-song.
⁶⁴Their priests fell by the sword;
And their widows made no lamentation.
⁶⁵Then the Lord awaked as one asleep,
Like a mighty man recovering from wine.
⁶⁶And He smote His adversaries backward;
He put upon them a perpetual reproach.
⁶⁷Moreover He abhorred the tent of Joseph,
And chose not the tribe of Ephraim;
⁶⁸But chose the tribe of Judah,
The mount Zion which He loved.
⁶⁹And He built His sanctuary like the heights,
Like the earth which He hath founded for ever.
⁷⁰He chose David also His servant,
And took him from the sheepfolds;
⁷¹From following the ewes that give suck He brought him,
To be shepherd over Jacob His people, and Israel His inheritance.
⁷²So he shepherded them according to the integrity of his heart;
And lead them by the skilfulness of his hands.

79 A Psalm of Asaph.

O God, the heathen are come into Thine inheritance;
They have defiled Thy holy temple;
They have made Jerusalem into heaps.
²They have given the dead bodies of Thy servants to be food unto the fowls of the heaven,
The flesh of Thy saints unto the beasts of the earth.
³They have shed their blood like water
Round about Jerusalem, with none to bury them.
⁴We are become a taunt to our neighbours,
A scorn and derision to them that are round about us.

[5]How long, O Lord, wilt Thou be angry for ever?
How long will Thy jealousy burn like fire?
[6]Pour out Thy wrath upon the nations that know Thee not,
And upon the kingdoms that call not upon Thy name.
[7]For they have devoured Jacob,
And laid waste his habitation.
[8]Remember not against us the iniquities of our forefathers;
Let Thy compassions speedily come to meet us;
For we are brought very low.
[9]Help us, O God of our salvation, for the sake of the glory of Thy name;
And deliver us, and forgive our sins, for Thy name's sake.
[10]Wherefore should the nations say: 'Where is their God?'
Let the avenging of Thy servants' blood that is shed
Be made known among the nations in our sight. [11]Let the groaning of the prisoner come before Thee;
According to the greatness of Thy power set free those that are appointed to death;
[12]And render unto our neighbours sevenfold into their bosom
Their reproach, wherewith they have reproached Thee, O Lord.
[13]So we that are Thy people and the flock of Thy pasture
Will give Thee thanks for ever;
We will tell of Thy praise to all generations.

80For the Leader; upon Shoshannim. A testimony. A Psalm of Asaph.

[2]Give ear, O Shepherd of Israel,
Thou that leadest Joseph like a flock;
Thou that art enthroned upon the cherubim, shine forth.
[3]Before Ephraim and Benjamin and Manasseh, stir up Thy might,
And come to save us.
[4]O God, restore us;
And cause Thy face to shine, and we shall be saved.
[5]O Lord God of hosts,
How long wilt Thou be angry against the prayer of Thy people?
[6]Thou hast fed them with the bread of tears,
And given them tears to drink in large measure.
[7]Thou makest us a strife unto our neighbours;
And our enemies mock as they please.
[8]O God of hosts, restore us;
And cause Thy face to shine, and we shall be saved.
[9]Thou didst pluck up a vine out of Egypt;
Thou didst drive out the nations, and didst plant it.
[10]Thou didst clear a place before it,
And it took deep root, and filled the land.
[11]The mountains were covered with the shadow of it,

And the mighty cedars with the boughs thereof.
¹²She sent out her branches unto the sea,
And her shoots unto the River.
¹³Why hast Thou broken down her fences,
So that all they that pass by the way do pluck her?
¹⁴The boar out of the wood doth ravage it,
That which moveth in the field feedeth on it.
¹⁵O God of hosts, return, we beseech Thee;
Look from heaven, and behold, and be mindful of this vine,
¹⁶And of the stock which Thy right hand hath planted,
And the branch that Thou madest strong for Thyself.
¹⁷It is burned with fire, it is cut down;
They perish at the rebuke of Thy countenance.
¹⁸Let Thy hand be upon the man of Thy right hand,
Upon the son of man whom Thou madest strong for Thyself.
¹⁹So shall we not turn back from Thee;
Quicken Thou us, and we will call upon Thy name.
²⁰O Lord God of hosts, restore us;
Cause Thy face to shine, and we shall be saved.

81For the Leader; upon the Gittith. [A Psalm] of Asaph.

²Sing aloud unto God our strength;
Shout unto the God of Jacob.
³Take up the melody, and sound the timbrel,
The sweet harp with the psaltery.
⁴Blow the horn at the new moon,
At the full moon for our feast-day.
⁵For it is a statute for Israel,
An ordinance of the God of Jacob.
⁶He appointed it in Joseph for a testimony,
When He went forth against the land of Egypt.
The speech of one that I knew not did I hear:
⁷'I removed his shoulder from the burden;
His hands were freed from the basket.
⁸Thou didst call in trouble, and I rescued thee;
I answered thee in the secret place of thunder;
I proved thee at the waters of Meribah.Selah
⁹Hear, O My people, and I will admonish thee:
O Israel, if thou wouldest hearken unto Me!
¹⁰There shall no strange god be in thee;
Neither shalt thou worship any foreign god.
¹¹I am the Lord thy God,
Who brought thee up out of the land of Egypt;

Open thy mouth wide, and I will fill it.
¹²But My people hearkened not to My voice;
And Israel would none of Me.
¹³So I let them go after the stubbornness of their heart,
That they might walk in their own counsels.
¹⁴Oh that My people would hearken unto Me,
That Israel would walk in My ways!
¹⁵I would soon subdue their enemies,
And turn My hand against their adversaries.
¹⁶The haters of the Lord should dwindle away before Him;
And their punishment should endure for ever.
¹⁷They should also be fed with the fat of wheat;
And with honey out of the rock would I satisfy thee.'

82A Psalm of Asaph.

God standeth in the congregation of God;
In the midst of the judges He judgeth:
²'How long will ye judge unjustly,
And respect the persons of the wicked?Selah
³Judge the poor and fatherless;
Do justice to the afflicted and destitute.
⁴Rescue the poor and needy;
Deliver them out of the hand of the wicked.
⁵They know not, neither do they understand;
They go about in darkness;
All the foundations of the earth are moved.
⁶I said: Ye are godlike beings,
And all of you sons of the Most High.
⁷Nevertheless ye shall die like men,
And fall like one of the princes.'
⁸Arise, O God, judge the earth;
For Thou shalt possess all the nations.

83A Song, a Psalm of Asaph.

²O God, keep not Thou silence;
Hold not Thy peace, and be not still, O God.
³For, lo, Thine enemies are in an uproar;
And they that hate Thee have lifted up the head.
⁴They hold crafty converse against Thy people,
And take counsel against Thy treasured ones.
⁵They have said: 'Come, and let us cut them off from being a nation;
That the name of Israel may be no more in remembrance.'

⁶For they have consulted together with one consent;
Against Thee do they make a covenant;
⁷The tents of Edom and the Ishmaelites;
Moab, and the Hagrites;
⁸Gebal, and Ammon, and Amalek;
Philistia with the inhabitants of Tyre;
⁹Assyria also is joined with them;
They have been an arm to the children of Lot.Selah
¹⁰Do Thou unto them as unto Midian;
As to Sisera, as to Jabin, at the brook Kishon;
¹¹Who were destroyed at En-dor;
They became as dung for the earth.
¹²Make their nobles like Oreb and Zeeb,
And like Zebah and Zalmunna all their princes;
¹³Who said: 'Let us take to ourselves in possession
The habitations of God.'
¹⁴O my God, make them like the whirling dust;
As stubble before the wind.
¹⁵As the fire that burneth the forest,
And as the flame that setteth the mountains ablaze;
¹⁶So pursue them with Thy tempest,
And affright them with Thy storm.
¹⁷Fill their faces with shame;
That they may seek Thy name, O LORD.
¹⁸Let them be ashamed and affrighted for ever;
Yea, let them be abashed and perish;
¹⁹That they may know that it is Thou alone whose name is the LORD,
The Most High over all the earth.

84For the Leader; upon the Gittith. A Psalm of the sons of Korah.

²How lovely are Thy tabernacles, O LORD of hosts!
³My soul yearneth, yea, even pineth for the courts of the LORD;
My heart and my flesh sing for joy unto the living God.
⁴Yea, the sparrow hath found a house, and the swallow a nest for herself,
Where she may lay her young;
Thine altars, O Lord of hosts,
My King, and my God—
⁵Happy are they that dwell in Thy house,
They are ever praising Thee.Selah
⁶Happy is the man whose strength is in Thee;
In whose heart are the highways.
⁷Passing through the valley of Baca they make it a place of springs;
Yea, the early rain clotheth it with blessings.

[8]They go from strength to strength,
Every one of them appeareth before God in Zion.
[9]O Lord God of hosts, hear my prayer;
Give ear, O God of Jacob.Selah
[10]Behold, O God our shield,
And look upon the face of Thine anointed.
[11]For a day in Thy courts is better than a thousand;
I had rather stand at the threshold of the house of my God,
Than to dwell in the tents of wickedness.
[12]For the Lord God is a sun and a shield;
The Lord giveth grace and glory;
No good thing will He withhold from them that walk uprightly.
[13]O Lord of hosts,
Happy is the man that trusteth in Thee.

85For the Leader. A Psalm of the sons of Korah.

[2]Lord, Thou hast been favourable unto Thy land,
Thou hast turned the captivity of Jacob.
[3]Thou hast forgiven the iniquity of Thy people,
Thou hast pardoned all their sin.Selah
[4]Thou hast withdrawn all Thy wrath;
Thou hast turned from the fierceness of Thine anger.
[5]Restore us, O God of our salvation,
And cause Thine indignation toward us to cease.
[6]Wilt Thou be angry with us for ever?
Wilt Thou draw out Thine anger to all generations?
[7]Wilt Thou not quicken us again,
That Thy people may rejoice in Thee?
[8]Show us Thy mercy, O Lord,
And grant us Thy salvation.
[9]I will hear what God the Lord will speak;
For He will speak peace unto His people, and to His saints;
But let them not turn back to folly.
[10]Surely His salvation is nigh them that fear Him;
That glory may dwell in our land.
[11]Mercy and truth are met together;
Righteousness and peace have kissed each other.
[12]Truth springeth out of the earth;
And righteousness hath looked down from heaven.
[13]Yea, the Lord will give that which is good;
And our land shall yield her produce.
[14]Righteousness shall go before Him,
And shall make His footsteps a way.

86A Prayer of David.

Incline Thine ear, O Lord, and answer me;
For I am poor and needy.
[2]Keep my soul, for I am godly;
O Thou my God, save Thy servant that trusteth in Thee.
[3]Be gracious unto me, O Lord;
For unto Thee do I cry all the day.
[4]Rejoice the soul of Thy servant;
For unto Thee, O Lord, do I lift up my soul.
[5]For Thou, Lord, art good, and ready to pardon,
And plenteous in mercy unto all them that call upon Thee.
[6]Give ear, O Lord, unto my prayer;
And attend unto the voice of my supplications.
[7]In the day of my trouble I call upon Thee;
For Thou wilt answer me.
[8]There is none like unto Thee among the gods, O Lord,
And there are no works like Thine.
[9]All nations whom Thou hast made shall come and prostrate themselves before Thee, O Lord;
And they shall glorify Thy name.
[10]For Thou art great, and doest wondrous things;
Thou art God alone.
[11]Teach me, O Lord, Thy way, that I may walk in Thy truth;
Make one my heart to fear Thy name.
[12]I will thank Thee, O Lord my God, with my whole heart;
And I will glorify Thy name for evermore.
[13]For great is Thy mercy toward me;
And Thou hast delivered my soul from the lowest nether-world.
[14]O God, the proud are risen up against me,
And the company of violent men have sought after my soul,
And have not set Thee before them.
[15]But Thou, O Lord, art a God full of compassion and gracious,
Slow to anger, and plenteous in mercy and truth.
[16]O turn unto me, and be gracious unto me;
Give Thy strength unto Thy servant,
And save the son of Thy handmaid.
[17]Work in my behalf a sign for good;
That they that hate me may see it, and be put to shame,
Because Thou, Lord, hast helped me, and comforted me.

87A Psalm of the sons of Korah; a Song.

His foundation is in the holy mountains.

²The Lord loveth the gates of Zion
More than all the dwellings of Jacob.
³Glorious things are spoken of Thee,
O city of God.Selah
⁴'I will make mention of Rahab and Babylon as among them that know Me;
Behold Philistia, and Tyre, with Ethiopia;
This one was born there.'
⁵But of Zion it shall be said: 'This man and that was born in her;
And the Most High Himself doth establish her.'
⁶The Lord shall count in the register of the peoples:
'This one was born there.'Selah
⁷And whether they sing or dance,
All my thoughts are in Thee.

88A Song, a Psalm of the sons of Korah; for the Leader; upon Mahalath Leannoth. Maschil of Heman the Ezrahite.

²O Lord, God of my salvation,
What time I cry in the night before Thee,
³Let my prayer come before Thee,
Incline Thine ear unto my cry.
⁴For my soul is sated with troubles,
And my life draweth nigh unto the grave.
⁵I am counted with them that go down into the pit;
I am become as a man that hath no help;
⁶Set apart among the dead,
Like the slain that lie in the grave,
Whom Thou rememberest no more;
And they are cut off from Thy hand.
⁷Thou hast laid me in the nethermost pit,
In dark places, in the deeps.
⁸Thy wrath lieth hard upon me,
And all Thy waves Thou pressest down.Selah
⁹Thou hast put mine acquaintance far from me;
Thou hast made me an abomination unto them;
I am shut up, and I cannot come forth.
¹⁰Mine eye languisheth by reason of affliction;
I have called upon Thee, O Lord, every day,
I have spread forth my hands unto Thee.
¹¹Wilt Thou work wonders for the dead?
Or shall the shades arise and give Thee thanks?Selah
¹²Shall Thy mercy be declared in the grave?
Or Thy faithfulness in destruction?
¹³Shall Thy wonders be known in the dark?

And Thy righteousness in the land of forgetfulness?
¹⁴But as for me, unto Thee, O Lord, do I cry,
And in the morning doth my prayer come to meet Thee.
¹⁵Lord, why castest Thou off my soul?
Why hidest Thou Thy face from me?
¹⁶I am afflicted and at the point of death from my youth up;
I have borne Thy terrors, I am distracted.
¹⁷Thy fierce wrath is gone over me;
Thy terrors have cut me off.
¹⁸They came round about me like water all the day;
They compassed me about together.
¹⁹Friend and companion hast Thou put far from me,
And mine acquaintance into darkness.

89Maschil of Ethan the Ezrahite.

²I will sing of the mercies of the Lord for ever;
To all generations will I make known Thy faithfulness with my mouth.
³For I have said: 'For ever is mercy built;
In the very heavens Thou dost establish Thy faithfulness.
⁴I have made a covenant with My chosen,
I have sworn unto David My servant:
⁵For ever will I establish thy seed,
And build up thy throne to all generations.'Selah
⁶So shall the heavens praise Thy wonders, O Lord,
Thy faithfulness also in the assembly of the holy ones.
⁷For who in the skies can be compared unto the Lord,
Who among the sons of might can be likened unto the Lord,
⁸A God dreaded in the great council of the holy ones,
And feared of all them that are about Him?
⁹O Lord God of hosts,
Who is a mighty one, like unto Thee, O Lord?
And Thy faithfulness is round about Thee.
¹⁰Thou rulest the proud swelling of the sea;
When the waves thereof arise, Thou stillest them.
¹¹Thou didst crush Rahab, as one that is slain;
Thou didst scattered Thine enemies with the arm of Thy strength.
¹²Thine are the heavens, Thine also the earth;
The world and the fulness thereof, Thou hast founded them.
¹³The north and the south, Thou hast created them;
Tabor and Hermon rejoice in Thy name.
¹⁴Thine is an arm with might;
Strong is Thy hand, and exalted is Thy right hand.
¹⁵Righteousness and justice are the foundation of Thy throne;

Mercy and truth go before Thee.

[16]Happy is the people that know the joyful shout;
They walk, O Lord, in the light of Thy countenance.

[17]In Thy name do they rejoice all the day;
And through Thy righteousness are they exalted.

[18]For Thou art the glory of their strength;
And in Thy favour our horn is exalted.

[19]For of the Lord is our shield;
And the Holy One of Israel is our king.

[20]Then Thou spokest in vision to Thy godly ones,
And saidst: 'I have laid help upon one that is mighty;
I have exalted one chosen out of the people.

[21]I have found David My servant;
With My holy oil have I anointed him;

[22]With whom My hand shall be established;
Mine arm also shall strengthen him.

[23]The enemy shall not exact from him;
Nor the son of wickedness afflict him.

[24]And I will beat to pieces his adversaries before him,
And smite them that hate him.

[25]But My faithfulness and My mercy shall be with him;
And through My name shall his horn be exalted.

[26]I will set his hand also on the sea,
And his right hand on the rivers.

[27]He shall call unto Me: Thou art my Father,
My God, and the rock of my salvation.

[28]I also will appoint him first-born,
The highest of the kings of the earth.

[29]For ever will I keep for him My mercy,
And My covenant shall stand fast with him.

[30]His seed also will I make to endure for ever,
And his throne as the days of heaven.

[31]If his children forsake My law,
And walk not in Mine ordinances;

[32]If they profane My statutes,
And keep not My commandments;

[33]Then will I visit their transgression with the rod,
And their iniquity with strokes.

[34]But My mercy will I not break off from him,
Nor will I be false to My faithfulness.

[35]My covenant will I not profane,
Nor alter that which is gone out of My lips.

[36]Once have I sworn by My holiness:
Surely I will not be false unto David;

³⁷His seed shall endure for ever,
And his throne as the sun before Me.
³⁸It shall be established for ever as the moon;
And be stedfast as the witness in sky.'Selah
³⁹But Thou hast cast off and rejected,
Thou hast been wroth with Thine anointed.
⁴⁰Thou hast abhorred the covenant of Thy servant;
Thou hast profaned his crown even to the ground.
⁴¹Thou hast broken down all his fences;
Thou hast brought his strongholds to ruin.
⁴²All that pass by the way spoil him;
He is become a taunt to his neighbours.
⁴³Thou hast exalted the right hand of his adversaries;
Thou hast made all his enemies to rejoice.
⁴⁴Yea, Thou turnest back the edge of his sword,
And hast not made him to stand in the battle.
⁴⁵Thou hast made his brightness to cease,
And cast his throne down to the ground.
⁴⁶The days of his youth hast Thou shortened;
Thou hast covered him with shame.Selah
⁴⁷How long, O Lord, wilt Thou hide Thyself for ever?
How long shall Thy wrath burn like fire?
⁴⁸O remember how short my time is;
For what vanity hast Thou created all the children of men!
⁴⁹What man is he that liveth and shall not see death,
That shall deliver his soul from the power of the grave?Selah
⁵⁰Where are Thy former mercies, O Lord,
Which Thou didst swear unto David in Thy faithfulness?
⁵¹Remember, Lord, the taunt of Thy servants;
How I do bear in my bosom [the taunt of] so many peoples;
⁵²Wherewith Thine enemies have taunted, O Lord,
Wherewith they have taunted the footsteps of Thine anointed.
⁵³Blessed be the Lord for evermore.
Amen, and Amen.

ספר רביעי
BOOK IV

90A Prayer of Moses the man of God.

Lord, Thou hast been our dwelling-place in all generations.
²Before the mountains were brought forth,
Or ever Thou hadst formed the earth and the world,
Even from everlasting to everlasting, Thou art God.

³Thou turnest man to contrition;
And sayest: 'Return, ye children of men.'
⁴For a thousand years in Thy sight
Are but as yesterday when it is past,
And as a watch in the night.
⁵Thou carriest them away as with a flood; they are as a sleep;
In the morning they are like grass which groweth up.
⁶In the morning it flourisheth, and groweth up;
In the evening it is cut down, and withereth.
⁷For we are consumed in Thine anger,
And by Thy wrath are we hurried away.
⁸Thou hast set our iniquities before Thee,
Our secret sins in the light of Thy countenance.
⁹For all our days are passed away in Thy wrath;
We bring our years to an end as a tale that is told.
¹⁰The days of our years are threescore years and ten,
Or even by reason of strength fourscore years;
Yet is their pride but travail and vanity;
For it is speedily gone, and we fly away.
¹¹Who knoweth the power of Thine anger,
And Thy wrath according to the fear that is due unto Thee?
¹²So teach us to number our days,
That we may get us a heart of wisdom.
¹³Return, O Lord; how long? And let it repent Thee concerning Thy servants.
¹⁴O satisfy us in the morning with Thy mercy;
That we may rejoice and be glad all our days.
¹⁵Make us glad according to the days wherein Thou hast afflicted us,
According to the years wherein we have seen evil.
¹⁶Let Thy work appear unto Thy servants,
And Thy glory upon their children.
¹⁷And let the graciousness of the Lord our God be upon us;
Establish Thou also upon us the work of our hands;
Yea, the work of our hands establish Thou it.

91O thou that dwellest in the covert of the Most High,
And abidest in the shadow of the Almighty;
²I will say of the Lord, who is my refuge and my fortress,
My God, in whom I trust,
³That He will deliver thee from the snare of the fowler,
And from the noisome pestilence.
⁴He will cover thee with His pinions,
And under His wings shalt thou take refuge;
His truth is a shield and a buckler.
⁵Thou shalt not be afraid of the terror by night,

Nor of the arrow that flieth by day;
[6]Of the pestilence that walketh in darkness,
Nor of the destruction that wasteth at noonday.
[7]A thousand may fall at Thy side,
And ten thousand at Thy right hand;
It shall not come nigh thee.
[8]Only with thine eyes shalt thou behold,
And see the recompense of the wicked.
[9]For thou hast made the Lord who is my refuge,
Even the Most High, thy habitation.
[10]There shall no evil befall thee,
Neither shall any plague come nigh thy tent.
[11]For He will give His angels charge over thee,
To keep thee in all thy ways.
[12]They shall bear thee upon their hands,
Lest thou dash thy foot against a stone.
[13]Thou shalt tread upon the lion and asp;
The young lion and the serpent shalt thou trample under feet.
[14]'Because he hath set his love upon Me, therefore will I deliver him;
I will set him on high, because he hath known My name.
[15]He shall call upon Me, and I will answer him; I will be with him in trouble;
I will rescue him, and bring him to honour.
[16]With long life will I satisfy him,
And make Him to behold My salvation.'

92A Psalm, a Song. For the sabbath day.

[2]It is a good thing to give thanks unto the Lord,
And to sing praises unto Thy name, O Most High;
[3]To declare Thy lovingkindness in the morning,
And Thy faithfulness in the night seasons,
[4]With an instrument of ten strings, and with the psaltery;
With a solemn sound upon the harp.
[5]For Thou, Lord, hast made me glad through Thy work;
I will exult in the works of Thy hands.
[6]How great are Thy works, O Lord!
Thy thoughts are very deep.
[7]A brutish man knoweth not,
Neither doth a fool understand this.
[8]When the wicked spring up as the grass,
And when all the workers of iniquity do flourish;
It is that they may be destroyed for ever.
[9]But Thou, O Lord, art on high for evermore.
[10]For, lo, Thine enemies, O Lord,

For, lo, Thine enemies shall perish:
All the workers of iniquity shall be scattered.
[11]But my horn hast Thou exalted like the horn of the wild-ox;
I am anointed with rich oil.
[12]Mine eye also hath gazed on them that lie in wait for me,
Mine ears have heard my desire of the evil-doers that rise up against me.
[13]The righteous shall flourish like the palm-tree;
He shall grow like a cedar in Lebanon.
[14]Planted in the house of the Lord,
They shall flourish in the courts of our God.
[15]They shall still bring forth fruit in old age;
They shall be full of sap and richness;
[16]To declare that the Lord is upright,
My Rock, in whom there is no unrighteousness.

93The Lord reigneth; He is clothed in majesty;
The Lord is clothed, He hath girded Himself with strength;
Yea, the world is established, that it cannot be moved.
[2]Thy throne is established of old;
Thou art from everlasting.
[3]The floods have lifted up, O Lord,
The floods have lifted up their voice;
The floods lift up their roaring.
[4]Above the voices of many waters,
The mighty breakers of the sea,
The Lord on high is mighty.
[5]Thy testimonies are very sure,
Holiness becometh Thy house,
O Lord, for evermore.

94O Lord, Thou God to whom vengeance belongeth,
Thou God to whom vengeance belongeth, shine forth.
[2]Lift up Thyself, Thou Judge of the earth;
Render to the proud their recompense.
[3]Lord, how long shall the wicked,
How long shall the wicked exult?
[4]They gush out, they speak arrogancy;
All the workers of iniquity bear themselves loftily.
[5]They crush Thy people, O Lord,
And afflict Thy heritage.
[6]They slay the widow and the stranger,
And murder the fatherless.
[7]And they say: 'The Lord will not see,
Neither will the God of Jacob give heed.'

⁸Consider, ye brutish among the people;
And ye fools, when will ye understand?
⁹He that planted the ear, shall He not hear?
He that formed the eye, shall He not see?
¹⁰He that instructeth nations, shall not He correct?
Even He that teacheth man knowledge?
¹¹The Lord knoweth the thoughts of man,
That they are vanity.
¹²Happy is the man whom Thou instructest, O Lord,
And teachest out of Thy law;
¹³That Thou mayest give him rest from the days of evil,
Until the pit be digged for the wicked.
¹⁴For the Lord will not cast off His people,
Neither will He forsake His inheritance.
¹⁵For right shall return unto justice,
And all the upright in heart shall follow it.
¹⁶Who will rise up for me against the evil-doers?
Who will stand up for me against the workers of iniquity?
¹⁷Unless the Lord had been my help,
My soul had soon dwelt in silence.
¹⁸If I say: 'My foot slippeth',
Thy mercy, O Lord, holdeth me up.
¹⁹When my cares are many within me, Thy comforts delight my soul.
²⁰Shall the seat of wickedness have fellowship with Thee,
Which frameth mischief by statute?
²¹They gather themselves together against the soul of the righteous,
And condemn innocent blood.
²²But the Lord hath been my high tower,
And my God the rock of my refuge.
²³And He hath brought upon them their own iniquity,
And will cut them off in their own evil;
The Lord our God will cut them off.

95O come, let us sing unto the Lord;
Let us shout for joy to the Rock of our salvation.
²Let us come before His presence with thanksgiving,
Let us shout for joy unto Him with psalms.
³For the Lord is a great God,
And a great King above all gods;
⁴In whose hand are the depths of the earth;
The heights of the mountains are His also.
⁵The sea is His, and He made it;
And His hands formed the dry land.
⁶O come, let us bow down and bend the knee;

Let us kneel before the Lord our Maker;
[7]For He is our God,
And we are the people of His pasture, and the flock of His hand.
To-day, if ye would but hearken to His voice!
[8]'Harden not your heart, as at Meribah,
As in the day of Massah in the wilderness;
[9]When your fathers tried Me,
Proved Me, even though they saw My work.
[10]For forty years was I wearied with that generation,
And said: It is a people that do err in their heart,
And they have not known My ways;
[11]Wherefore I swore in My wrath,
That they should not enter into My [3]rest.'

96 O sing unto the Lord a new song;
Sing unto the Lord, all the earth.
[2]Sing unto the Lord, bless His name;
Proclaim His salvation from day to day.
[3]Declare His glory among the nations,
His marvellous works among all the peoples.
[4]For great is the Lord, and highly to be praised;
He is to be feared above all gods.
[5]For all the gods of the peoples are things of nought;
But the Lord made the heavens.
[6]Honour and majesty are before Him;
Strength and beauty are in His sanctuary.
[7]Ascribe unto the Lord, ye kindreds of the peoples,
Ascribe unto the Lord glory and strength.
[8]Ascribe unto the Lord the glory due unto His name;
Bring an offering, and come into His courts.
[9]O worship the Lord in the beauty of holiness;
Tremble before Him, all the earth.
[10]Say among the nations: 'The Lord reigneth.'
The world also is established that it cannot be moved;
He will judge the peoples with equity.
[11]Let the heavens be glad, and let the earth rejoice;
Let the sea roar, and the fulness thereof;
[12]Let the field exult; and all that is therein;
Then shall all the trees of the wood sing for joy;
[13]Before the Lord, for He is come;
For He is come to judge the earth;
He will judge the world with righteousness,
And the peoples in His faithfulness.

97The Lord reigneth; let the earth rejoice;
Let the multitude of isles be glad.
2Clouds and darkness are round about Him;
Righteousness and justice are the foundation of His throne.
3A fire goeth before Him,
And burneth up His adversaries round about.
4His lightnings lighted up the world;
The earth saw, and trembled.
5The mountains melted like wax at the presence of the Lord,
At the presence of the Lord of the whole earth.
6The heavens declared His righteousness,
And all the peoples saw His glory.
7Ashamed be all they that serve graven images,
That boast themselves of things of nought;
Bow down to Him, all ye gods.
8Zion heard and was glad,
And the daughters of Judah rejoiced;
Because of Thy judgments, O Lord.
9For Thou, Lord, art most high above all the earth;
Thou art exalted far above all gods.
10O ye that love the Lord, hate evil;
He preserveth the souls of His saints; He delivered them out of the hand of the wicked.
11Light is sown for the righteous,
And gladness for the upright in heart.
12Be glad in the Lord, ye righteous;
And give thanks to His holy name.

98A Psalm.

O sing unto the Lord a new song;
For He hath done marvellous things;
His right hand, and His holy arm, hath wrought salvation for Him.
2The Lord hath made known His salvation;
His righteousness hath He revealed in the sight of the nations.
3He hath remembered His mercy and His faithfulness toward the house of Israel;
All the ends of the earth have seen the salvation of our God.
4Shout unto the Lord, all the earth;
Break forth and sing for joy, yea, sing praises.
5Sing praises unto the Lord with the harp;
With the harp and the voice of melody.
6With trumpets and sound of the horn
Shout ye before the King, the Lord.
7Let the sea roar, and the fulness thereof;
The world, and they that dwell therein;

⁸Let the floods clap their hands;
Let the mountains sing for joy together;
⁹Before the Lord, for He is come to judge the earth;
He will judge the world with righteousness,
And the peoples with equity.

99The Lord reigneth; let the peoples tremble;
He is enthroned upon the cherubim; let the earth quake.
²The Lord is great in Zion;
And He is high above all the peoples.
³Let them praise Thy name as great and awful;
Holy is He.
⁴The strength also of the king who loveth justice—
Thou hast established equity,
Thou hast executed justice and righteousness in Jacob.
⁵Exalt ye the Lord our God,
And prostrate yourselves at His footstool;
Holy is He.
⁶Moses and Aaron among His priests,
And Samuel among them that call upon His name,
Did call upon the Lord, and He answered them.
⁷He spoke unto them in the pillar of cloud;
They kept His testimonies, and the statute that He gave them.
⁸O Lord our God, Thou didst answer them;
A forgiving God wast Thou unto them,
Though Thou tookest vengeance of their misdeeds.
⁹Exalt ye the Lord our God,
And worship at His holy hill;
For the Lord our God is holy.

100A Psalm of thanksgiving.

Shout unto the Lord, all the earth.
²Serve the Lord with gladness;
Come before His presence with singing.
³Know ye that the Lord He is God;
It is He that hath made us, and we are His,
His people, and the flock of His pasture.
⁴Enter into His gates with thanksgiving,
And into His courts with praise;
Give thanks unto Him, and bless His name.
⁵For the Lord is good; His mercy endureth for ever;
And His faithfulness unto all generations.

101A Psalm of David.

I will sing of mercy and justice;
Unto Thee, O Lord, will I sing praises.
²I will give heed unto the way of integrity;
Oh when wilt Thou come unto me?
I will walk within my house in the integrity of my heart.
³I will set no base thing before mine eyes;
I hate the doing of things crooked; it shall not cleave unto me.
⁴A perverse heart shall depart from me;
I will know no evil thing.
⁵Whoso slandereth his neighbour in secret, him will I destroy;
Whoso is haughty of eye and proud of heart, him will I not suffer.
⁶Mine eyes are upon the faithful of the land, that they may dwell with me;
He that walketh in a way of integrity, he shall minister unto me.
⁷He that worketh deceit shall not dwell within my house;
He that speaketh falsehood shall not be established before mine eyes.
⁸Morning by morning will I destroy all the wicked of the land;
To cut off all the workers of iniquity from the city of the Lord.
102A Prayer of the afflicted, when he fainteth, and poureth out his complaint before the Lord.
²O Lord, hear my prayer,
And let my cry come unto Thee.
³Hide not Thy face from me in the day of my distress;
Incline Thine ear unto me;
In the day when I call answer me speedily.
⁴For my days are consumed like smoke,
And my bones are burned as a hearth.
⁵My heart is smitten like grass, and withered;
For I forget to eat my bread.
⁶By reason of the voice of my sighing
My bones cleave to my flesh.
⁷I am like a pelican of the wilderness;
I am become as an owl of the waste places.
⁸I watch, and am become
Like a sparrow that is alone upon the housetop.
⁹Mine enemies taunt me all the day;
They that are mad against me do curse by me.
¹⁰For I have eaten ashes like bread,
And mingled my drink with weeping,
¹¹Because of Thine indignation and Thy wrath;
For Thou hast taken me up, and cast me away.
¹²My days are like a lengthening shadow;
And I am withered like grass.
¹³But Thou, O Lord, sittest enthroned for ever;

And Thy name is unto all generations.
¹⁴Thou wilt arise, and have compassion upon Zion;
For it is time to be gracious unto her, for the appointed time is come.
¹⁵For Thy servants take pleasure in her stones,
And love her dust.
¹⁶So the nations will fear the name of the Lord,
And all the kings of the earth Thy glory;
¹⁷When the Lord hath built up Zion,
When He hath appeared in His glory;
¹⁸When He hath regarded the prayer of the destitute,
And hath not despised their prayer.
¹⁹This shall be written for the generation to come;
And a people which shall be created shall praise the Lord.
²⁰For He hath looked down from the height of His sanctuary;
From heaven did the Lord behold the earth;
²¹To hear the groaning of the prisoner;
To loose those that are appointed to death;
²²That men may tell of the name of the Lord in Zion,
And His praise in Jerusalem;
²³When the peoples are gathered together,
And the kingdoms, to serve the Lord.
²⁴He weakened my strength in the way;
He shortened my days.
²⁵I say: 'O my God, take me not away in the midst of my days,
Thou whose years endure throughout all generations.
²⁶Of old Thou didst lay the foundation of the earth;
And the heavens are the work of Thy hands.
²⁷They shall perish, but Thou shalt endure;
Yea, all of them shall wax old like a garment;
As a vesture shalt Thou change them, and they shall pass away;
²⁸But Thou art the selfsame,
And Thy years shall have no end.
²⁹The children of Thy servants shall dwell securely,
And their seed shall be established before Thee.'

103[A Psalm] of David.

Bless the Lord, O my soul;
And all that is within me, bless His holy name.
²Bless the Lord, O my soul,
And forget not all His benefits;
³Who forgiveth all thine iniquity;
Who healeth all Thy diseases;
⁴Who redeemeth Thy life from the pit;

Who encompasseth thee with lovingkindness and tender mercies;
⁵Who satisfieth thine old age with good things;
So that Thy youth is renewed like the eagle.
⁶The Lord executeth righteousness,
And acts of justice for all that are oppressed.
⁷He made known His ways unto Moses,
His doings unto the children of Israel.
⁸The Lord is full of compassion and gracious,
Slow to anger, and plenteous in mercy.
⁹He will not always contend;
Neither will He keep His anger for ever.
¹⁰He hath not dealt with us after our sins,
Nor requited us according to our iniquities.
¹¹For as the heaven is high above the earth,
So great is His mercy toward them that fear Him.
¹²As far as the east is from the west,
So far hath He removed our transgressions from us.
¹³Like as a father hath compassion upon his children,
So hath the Lord compassion upon them that fear Him. ¹⁴For He knoweth our frame;
He remembereth that we are dust.
¹⁵As for man, his days are as grass;
As a flower of the field, so he flourisheth.
¹⁶For the wind passeth over it, and it is gone;
And the place thereof knoweth it no more.
¹⁷But the mercy of the Lord is from everlasting to everlasting upon them that fear Him,
And His righteousness unto children's children;
¹⁸To such as keep His covenant,
And to those that remember His precepts to do them.
¹⁹The Lord hath established His throne in the heavens;
And His kingdom ruleth over all.
²⁰Bless the Lord, ye angels of His,
Ye mighty in strength, that fulfil His word,
Hearkening unto the voice of His word.
²¹Bless the Lord, all ye His hosts;
Ye ministers of His, that do His pleasure.
²²Bless the Lord, all ye His works,
In all places of His dominion;
Bless the Lord, O my soul.
104Bless the Lord, O my soul.
O Lord my God, Thou art very great;
Thou art clothed with glory and majesty.
²Who coverest Thyself with light as with a garment,
Who stretchest out the heavens like a curtain;
³Who layest the beams of Thine upper chambers in the waters,

Who makest the clouds Thy chariot,
Who walkest upon the wings of the wind;
4Who makest winds Thy messengers,
The flaming fire Thy ministers.
5Who didst establish the earth upon its foundations,
That it should not be moved for ever and ever;
6Thou didst cover it with the deep as with a vesture;
The waters stood above the mountains.
7At Thy rebuke they fled,
At the voice of Thy thunder they hasted away—
8The mountains rose, the valleys sank down—
Unto the place which Thou hadst founded for them;
9Thou didst set a bound which they should not pass over,
That they might not return to cover the earth.
10Who sendest forth springs into the valleys;
They run between the mountains;
11They give drink to every beast of the field,
The wild asses quench their thirst.
12Beside them dwell the fowl of the heaven,
From among the branches they sing.
13Who waterest the mountains from Thine upper chambers;
The earth is full of the fruit of Thy works.
14Who causeth the grass to spring up for the cattle,
And herb for the service of man;
To bring forth bread out of the earth,
15And wine that maketh glad the heart of man,
Making the face brighter than oil,
And bread that stayeth man's heart.
16The trees of the Lord have their fill,
The cedars of Lebanon, which He hath planted;
17Wherein the birds make their nests;
As for the stork, the fir-trees are her house.
18The high mountains are for the wild goats;
The rocks are a refuge for the conies.
19Who appointedst the moon for seasons;
The sun knoweth his going down.
20Thou makest darkness, and it is night,
Wherein all the beasts of the forest do creep forth.
21The young lions roar after their prey,
And seek their food from God.
22The sun ariseth, they slink away,
And couch in their dens.
23Man goeth forth unto his work
And to his labour until the evening.

[24]How manifold are Thy works, O Lord!
In wisdom hast Thou made them all;
The earth is full of Thy creatures.
[25]Yonder sea, great and wide,
Therein are creeping things innumerable,
Living creatures, both small and great.
[26]There go the ships;
There is leviathan, whom Thou hast formed to sport therein.
[27]All of them wait for Thee,
That Thou mayest give them their food in due season.
[28]Thou givest it unto them, they gather it;
Thou openest Thy hand, they are satisfied with good.
[29]Thou hidest Thy face, they vanish;
Thou withdrawest their breath, they perish,
And return to their dust.
[30]Thou sendest forth Thy spirit, they are created;
And Thou renewest the face of the earth.
[31]May the glory of the Lord endure for ever;
Let the Lord rejoice in His works!
[32]Who looketh on the earth, and it trembleth;
He toucheth the mountains, and they smoke.
[33]I will sing unto the Lord as long as I live;
I will sing praise to my God while I have any being.
[34]Let my musing be sweet unto Him;
As for me, I will rejoice in the Lord.
[35]Let sinners cease out of the earth,
And let the wicked be no more.
Bless the Lord, O my soul.
[4]Hallelujah.

105O give thanks unto the Lord, call upon His name;
Make known His doings among the peoples.
[2]Sing unto Him, sing praises unto Him;
Speak ye of all His marvellous works.
[3]Glory ye in His holy name;
Let the heart of them rejoice that seek the Lord.
[4]Seek ye the Lord and His strength;
Seek His face continually.
[5]Remember His marvellous works that He hath done,
His wonders, and the judgments of His mouth;
[6]O ye seed of Abraham His servant,
Ye children of Jacob, His chosen ones.
[7]He is the Lord our God;
His judgments are in all the earth.

⁸He hath remembered His covenant for ever,
The word which He commanded to a thousand generations;
⁹[The covenant] which He made with Abraham,
And His oath unto Isaac;
¹⁰And He established it unto Jacob for a statute,
To Israel for an everlasting covenant;
¹¹Saying: 'Unto thee will I give the land of Canaan,
The lot of your inheritance.'
¹²When they were but a few men in number.
Yea, very few, and sojourners in it,
¹³And when they went about from nation to nation,
From one kingdom to another people,
¹⁴He suffered no man to do them wrong,
Yea, for their sake He reproved kings:
¹⁵'Touch not Mine anointed ones,
And do My prophets no harm.'
¹⁶And He called a famine upon the land;
He broke the whole staff of bread.
¹⁷He sent a man before them;
Joseph was sold for a servant;
¹⁸His feet they hurt with fetters,
His person was laid in iron;
¹⁹Until the time that his word came to pass, The word of the Lord tested him.
²⁰The king sent and loosed him;
Even the ruler of the peoples, and set him free.
²¹He made him lord of his house,
And ruler of all his possessions;
²²To bind his princes at his pleasure,
And teach his elders wisdom.
²³Israel also came into Egypt;
And Jacob sojourned in the land of Ham.
²⁴And He increased His people greatly,
And made them too mighty for their adversaries.
²⁵He turned their heart to hate His people,
To deal craftily with His servants.
²⁶He sent Moses His servant,
And Aaron whom He had chosen.
²⁷They wrought among them His manifold signs,
And wonders in the land of Ham.
²⁸He sent darkness, and it was dark;
And they rebelled not against His word.
²⁹He turned their waters into blood,
And slew their fish.
³⁰Their land swarmed with frogs,

In the chambers of their kings.
³¹He spoke, and there came swarms of flies,
And gnats in all their borders.
³²He gave them hail for rain,
And flaming fire in their land.
³³He smote their vines also and their fig-trees;
And broke the trees of their borders.
³⁴He spoke, and the locust came,
And the canker-worm without number,
³⁵And did eat up every herb in their land,
And did eat up the fruit of their ground.
³⁶He smote also all the first-born in their land,
The first-fruits of all their strength.
³⁷And He brought them forth with silver and gold;
And there was none that stumbled among His tribes.
³⁸Egypt was glad when they departed;
For the fear of them had fallen upon them.
³⁹He spread a cloud for a screen;
And fire to give light in the night.
⁴⁰They asked, and He brought quails,
And gave them in plenty the bread of heaven.
⁴¹He opened the rock, and waters gushed out;
They ran, a river in the dry places.
⁴²For He remembered His holy word
Unto Abraham His servant;
⁴³And He brought forth His people with joy,
His chosen ones with singing.
⁴⁴And He gave them the lands of the nations,
And they took the labour of the peoples in possession;
⁴⁵That they might keep His statutes,
And observe His laws.
Hallelujah.

106Hallelujah.
O give thanks unto the Lord; for He is good;
For His mercy endureth for ever.
²Who can express the mighty acts of the Lord,
Or make all His praise to be heard?
³Happy are they that keep justice,
That do righteousness at all times.
⁴Remember me, O Lord, when Thou favourest Thy people;
O think of me at Thy salvation;
⁵That I may behold the prosperity of Thy chosen,
That I may rejoice in the gladness of Thy nation,

That I may glory with Thine inheritance.
⁶We have sinned with our fathers,
We have done iniquitously, we have dealt wickedly.
⁷Our fathers in Egypt gave no heed unto Thy wonders;
They remembered not the multitude of Thy mercies;
But were rebellious at the sea, even at the Red Sea.
⁸Nevertheless He saved them for His name's sake,
That He might make His mighty power to be known.
⁹And He rebuked the Red Sea, and it was dried up;
And He led them through the depths, as through a wilderness.
¹⁰And He saved them from the hand of him that hated them,
And redeemed them from the hand of the enemy.
¹¹And the waters covered their adversaries;
There was not one of them left.
¹²Then believed they His words;
They sang His praise.
¹³They soon forgot His works;
They waited not for His counsel;
¹⁴But lusted exceedingly in the wilderness,
And tried God in the desert.
¹⁵And He gave them their request;
But sent leanness into their soul.
¹⁶They were jealous also of Moses in the camp,
And of Aaron the holy one of the Lord.
¹⁷The earth opened and swallowed up Dathan,
And covered the company of Abiram.
¹⁸And a fire was kindled in their company;
The flame burned up the wicked.
¹⁹They made a calf in Horeb,
And worshipped a molten image.
²⁰Thus they exchanged their glory
For the likeness of an ox that eateth grass.
²¹They forgot God their saviour,
Who had done great things in Egypt;
²²Wondrous works in the land of Ham, Terrible things by the Red Sea.
²³Therefore He said that He would destroy them,
Had not Moses His chosen stood before Him in the breach,
To turn back His wrath, lest He should destroy them.
²⁴Moreover, they scorned the desirable land,
They believed not His word;
²⁵And they murmured in their tents,
They hearkened not unto the voice of the Lord.
²⁶Therefore He swore concerning them,
That He would overthrow them in the wilderness;

²⁷And that He would cast out their seed among the nations,
And scatter them in the lands.
²⁸They joined themselves also unto Baal of Peor,
And ate the sacrifices of the dead.
²⁹Thus they provoked Him with their doings,
And the plague broke in upon them.
³⁰Then stood up Phinehas, and wrought judgment,
And so the plague was stayed.
³¹And that was counted unto him for righteousness,
Unto all generations for ever.
³²They angered Him also at the waters of Meribah,
And it went ill with Moses because of them;
³³For they embittered his spirit,
And he spoke rashly with his lips.
³⁴They did not destroy the peoples,
As the Lord commanded them;
³⁵But mingled themselves with the nations,
And learned their works;
³⁶And they served their idols,
Which became a snare unto them;
³⁷Yea, they sacrificed their sons and their daughters unto demons,
³⁸And shed innocent blood, even the blood of their sons and of their daughters,
Whom they sacrificed unto the idols of Canaan;
And the land was polluted with blood.
³⁹Thus were they defiled with their works,
And went astray in their doings.
⁴⁰Therefore was the wrath of the Lord kindled against His people,
And He abhorred His inheritance.
⁴¹And He gave them into the hand of the nations;
And they that hated them ruled over them.
⁴²Their enemies also oppressed them,
And they were subdued under their hand.
⁴³Many times did He deliver them;
But they were rebellious in their counsel,
And sank low through their iniquity.
⁴⁴Nevertheless He looked upon their distress,
When He heard their cry;
⁴⁵And He remembered for them His covenant,
And repented according to the multitude of His mercies.
⁴⁶He made them also to be pitied
Of all those that carried them captive.
⁴⁷Save us, O Lord our God,
And gather us from among the nations,
That we may give thanks unto Thy holy name,

That we may triumph in Thy praise.
⁴⁸Blessed be the Lord, the God of Israel,
From everlasting even to everlasting,
And let all the people say: 'Amen.'
Hallelujah.

ספר חמישי
BOOK V

107'O give thanks unto the Lord, for He is good,
For His mercy endureth for ever.'
²So let the redeemed of the Lord say,
Whom He hath redeemed from the hand of the adversary;
³And gathered them out of the lands,
From the east and from the west,
From the north and from the sea.
⁴They wandered in the wilderness in a desert way;
They found no city of habitation.
⁵Hungry and thirsty,
Their soul fainted in them.
⁶Then they cried unto the Lord in their trouble,
And He delivered them out of their distresses.
⁷And He led them by a straight way,
That they might go to a city of habitation.
⁸Let them give thanks unto the Lord for His mercy,
And for His wonderful works to the children of men!
⁹For He hath satisfied the longing soul,
And the hungry soul He hath filled with good.
¹⁰Such as sat in darkness and in the shadow of death,
Being bound in affliction and iron—
¹¹Because they rebelled against the words of God,
And contemned the counsel of the Most High.
¹²Therefore He humbled their heart with travail,
They stumbled, and there was none to help—
¹³They cried unto the Lord in their trouble,
And He saved them out of their distresses.
¹⁴He brought them out of darkness and the shadow of death,
And broke their bands in sunder. ¹⁵Let them give thanks unto the Lord for His mercy,
And for His wonderful works to the children of men!
¹⁶For He hath broken the gates of brass,
And cut the bars of iron in sunder.
¹⁷Crazed because of the way of their transgression,
And afflicted because of their iniquities—
¹⁸Their soul abhorred all manner of food,

And they drew near unto the gates of death—
[19]They cried unto the Lord in their trouble,
And He saved them out of their distresses;
[20]He sent His word, and healed them,
And delivered them from their graves.
[21]Let them give thanks unto the Lord for His mercy,
And for His wonderful works to the children of men!
[22]And let them offer the sacrifices of thanksgiving,
And declare His works with singing.
[23]They that go down to the sea in ships,
That do business in great waters—
[24]These saw the works of the Lord,
And His wonders in the deep;
[25]For He commanded, and raised the stormy wind,
Which lifted up the waves thereof;
[26]They mounted up to the heaven, they went down to the deeps;
Their soul melted away because of trouble;
[27]They reeled to and fro, and staggered like a drunken man,
And all their wisdom was swallowed up—
[28]They cried unto the Lord in their trouble,
And He brought them out of their distresses.
[29]He made the storm a calm,
So that the waves thereof were still.
[30]Then were they glad because they were quiet,
And He led them unto their desired haven.
[31]Let them give thanks unto the Lord for His mercy,
And for His wonderful works to the children of men!
[32]Let them exalt Him also in the assembly of the people,
And praise Him in the seat of the elders.
[33]He turneth rivers into a wilderness,
And watersprings into a thirsty ground;
[34]A fruitful land into a salt waste,
For the wickedness of them that dwell therein.
[35]He turneth a wilderness into a pool of water,
And a dry land into watersprings.
[36]And there He maketh the hungry to dwell,
And they establish a city of habitation;
[37]And sow fields, and plant vineyards,
Which yield fruits of increase.
[38]He blesseth them also, so that they are multiplied greatly,
And suffereth not their cattle to decrease.
[39]Again, they are minished and dwindle away
Through oppression of evil and sorrow.
[40]He poureth contempt upon princes,

And causeth them to wander in the waste, where there is no way.
⁴¹Yet setteth He the needy on high from affliction,
And maketh his families like a flock.
⁴²The upright see it, and are glad;
And all iniquity stoppeth her mouth.
⁴³Whoso is wise, let him observe these things,
And let them consider the mercies of the Lord.

108A Song, a Psalm of David.

²My heart is steadfast, O God;
I will sing, yea, I will sing praises, even with my glory.
³Awake, psaltery and harp;
I will awake the dawn.
⁴I will give thanks unto Thee, O Lord, among the peoples;
And I will sing praises unto Thee among the nations.
⁵For Thy mercy is great above the heavens,
And Thy truth reacheth unto the skies.
⁶Be Thou exalted, O God, above the heavens;
And Thy glory be above all the earth.
⁷That Thy beloved may be delivered,
Save with Thy right hand, and answer me.
⁸God spoke in His holiness, that I would exult;
That I would divide Shechem, and mete out the valley of Succoth.
⁹Gilead is mine, Manasseh is mine;
Ephraim also is the defence of my head;
Judah is my sceptre.
¹⁰Moab is my washpot;
Upon Edom do I cast my shoe;
Over Philistia do I cry aloud.
¹¹Who will bring me into the fortified city?
Who will lead me unto Edom?
¹²Hast not Thou cast us off, O God?
And Thou goest not forth, O God, with our hosts?
¹³Give us help against the adversary;
For vain is the help of man.
¹⁴Through God we shall do valiantly;
For He it is that will tread down our adversaries.

109For the Leader. A Psalm of David.

O God of my praise, keep not silence;
²For the mouth of the wicked and the mouth of deceit have they opened against me;
They have spoken unto me with a lying tongue.

³They compassed me about also with words of hatred,
And fought against me without a cause.
⁴In return for my love they are my adversaries;
But I am all prayer.
⁵And they have laid upon me evil for good,
And hatred for my love:
⁶'Set Thou a wicked man over him;
And let an adversary stand at his right hand.
⁷When he is judged, let him go forth condemned;
And let his prayer be turned into sin.
⁸Let his days be few;
Let another take his charge.
⁹Let his children be fatherless,
And his wife a widow.
¹⁰Let his children be vagabonds, and beg;
And let them seek their bread out of their desolate places.
¹¹Let the creditor distrain all that he hath;
And let strangers make spoil of his labour.
¹²Let there be none to extend kindness unto him;
Neither let there be any to be gracious unto his fatherless children.
¹³Let his posterity be cut off;
In the generation following let their name be blotted out.
¹⁴Let the iniquity of his fathers be brought to remembrance unto the Lord;
And let not the sin of his mother be blotted out.
¹⁵Let them be before the Lord continually,
That He may cut off the memory of them from the earth.
¹⁶Because that he remembered not to do kindness,
But persecuted the poor and needy man,
And the broken in heart he was ready to slay.
¹⁷Yea, he loved cursing, and it came unto him;
And he delighted not in blessing, and it is far from him.
¹⁸He clothed himself also with cursing as with his raiment,
And it is come into his inward parts like water,
And like oil into his bones.
¹⁹Let it be unto him as the garment which he putteth on,
And for the girdle wherewith he is girded continually.'
²⁰This would mine adversaries effect from the Lord,
And they that speak evil against my soul.
²¹But Thou, O God the Lord, deal with me for Thy name's sake;
Because Thy mercy is good, deliver Thou me.
²²For I am poor and needy,
And my heart is wounded within me.
²³I am gone like the shadow when it lengtheneth;
I am shaken off as the locust.

²⁴My knees totter through fasting;
And my flesh is lean, and hath no fatness.
²⁵I am become also a taunt unto them;
When they see me, they shake their head.
²⁶Help me, O Lord my God;
O save me according to Thy mercy;
²⁷That they may know that this is Thy hand;
That Thou, Lord, hast done it.
²⁸Let them curse, but bless Thou;
When they arise, they shall be put to shame, but Thy servant shall rejoice.
²⁹Mine adversaries shall be clothed with confusion,
And shall put on their own shame as a robe.
³⁰I will give great thanks unto the Lord with my mouth;
Yea, I will praise Him among the multitude;
³¹Because He standeth at the right hand of the needy,
To save him from them that judge his soul.

110A Psalm of David.

The Lord saith unto my lord: 'Sit thou at My right hand,
Until I make thine enemies thy footstool.'
²The rod of Thy strength the Lord will send out of Zion:
'Rule thou in the midst of thine enemies.'
³Thy people offer themselves willingly in the day of thy warfare;
In adornments of holiness, from the womb of the dawn,
Thine is the dew of thy youth.
⁴The Lord hath sworn, and will not repent:
'Thou art a priest for ever
After the manner of Melchizedek.'
⁵The Lord at thy right hand
Doth crush kings in the day of His wrath.
⁶He will judge among the nations;
He filleth it with the dead bodies,
He crusheth the head over a wide land.
⁷He will drink of the brook in the way;
Therefore will he lift up the head.

111Hallelujah.

אI will give thanks unto the Lord with my whole heart,
בIn the council of the upright, and in the congregation.
²גThe works of the Lord are great,
דSought out of all them that have delight therein.
³הHis work is glory and majesty;

וAnd His righteousness endureth for ever.
⁴זHe hath made a memorial for His wonderful works;
חThe Lord is gracious and full of compassion.
⁵טHe hath given food unto them that fear Him;
יHe will ever be mindful of His covenant.
⁶כHe hath declared to His people the power of His works,
לIn giving them the heritage of the nations.
⁷מThe works of His hands are truth and justice;
נAll His precepts are sure.
⁸סThey are established for ever and ever,
עThey are done in truth and uprightness.
⁹פHe hath sent redemption unto His people;
צHe hath commanded His covenant for ever;
קHoly and awful is His name.
¹⁰רThe fear of the Lord is the beginning of wisdom;
שA good understanding have all they that do thereafter;
תHis praise endureth for ever.

112Hallelujah.

אHappy is the man that feareth the Lord,
בThat delighteth greatly in His commandments.
²גHis seed shall be mighty upon earth;
דThe generation of the upright shall be blessed.
³הWealth and riches are in his house;
וAnd his merit endureth for ever.
⁴זUnto the upright He shineth as a light in the darkness,
חGracious, and full of compassion, and righteous.
⁵טWell is it with the man that dealeth graciously and lendeth,
יThat ordereth his affairs rightfully.
⁶כFor he shall never be moved;
לThe righteous shall be had in everlasting remembrance.
⁷מHe shall not be afraid of evil tidings;
נHis heart is stedfast, trusting in the Lord.
⁸סHis heart is established, he shall not be afraid,
עUntil he gaze upon his adversaries.
⁹פHe hath scattered abroad, he hath given to the needy;
צHis righteousness endureth for ever;
קHis horn shall be exalted in honour.
¹⁰רThe wicked shall see it, and be vexed;
שHe shall gnash with his teeth, and melt away;
תThe desire of the wicked shall perish.

113Hallelujah.

Praise, O ye servants of the Lord,
Praise the name of the Lord.
²Blessed be the name of the Lord
From this time forth and for ever.
³From the rising of the sun unto the going down thereof
The Lord's name is to be praised.
⁴The Lord is high above all nations,
His glory is above the heavens.
⁵Who is like unto the Lord our God,
That is enthroned on high,
⁶That looketh down low
Upon heaven and upon the earth?
⁷Who raiseth up the poor out of the dust,
And lifteth up the needy out of the dunghill;
⁸That He may set him with princes,
Even with the princes of His people.
⁹Who maketh the barren woman to dwell in her house
As a joyful mother of children.
Hallelujah.

114When Israel came forth out of Egypt,
The house of Jacob from a people of strange language;
²Judah became His sanctuary,
Israel His dominion.
³The sea saw it, and fled;
The Jordan turned backward.
⁴The mountains skipped like rams,
The hills like young sheep.
⁵What aileth thee, O thou sea, that thou fleest?
Thou Jordan, that thou turnest backward?
⁶Ye mountains, that ye skip like rams;
Ye hills, like young sheep?
⁷Tremble, thou earth, at the presence of the Lord,
At the presence of the God of Jacob;
⁸Who turned the rock into a pool of water,
The flint into a fountain of waters.

115Not unto us, O Lord, not unto us,
But unto Thy name give glory,
For Thy mercy, and for Thy truth's sake.
²Wherefore should the nations say:
'Where is now their God?'
³But our God is in the heavens;
Whatsoever pleased Him He hath done.

⁴Their idols are silver and gold,
The work of men's hands.
⁵They have mouths, but they speak not;
Eyes have they, but they see not;
⁶They have ears, but they hear not;
Noses have they, but they smell not;
⁷They have hands, but they handle not;
Feet have they, but they walk not;
Neither speak they with their throat.
⁸They that make them shall be like unto them;
Yea, every one that trusteth in them.
⁹O Israel, trust thou in the Lord!
He is their help and their shield!
¹⁰O house of Aaron, trust ye in the Lord!
He is their help and their shield!
¹¹Ye that fear the Lord, trust in the Lord!
He is their help and their shield.
¹²The Lord hath been mindful of us, He will bless—
He will bless the house of Israel;
He will bless the house of Aaron.
¹³He will bless them that fear the Lord,
Both small and great.
¹⁴The Lord increase you more and more,
You and your children.
¹⁵Blessed be ye of the Lord
Who made heaven and earth.
¹⁶The heavens are the heavens of the Lord;
But the earth hath He given to the children of men.
¹⁷The dead praise not the Lord,
Neither any that go down into silence;
¹⁸But we will bless the Lord
From this time forth and for ever.
Hallelujah.

116I love that the Lord should hear
My voice and my supplications.
²Because He hath inclined His ear unto me,
Therefore will I call upon Him all my days.
³The cords of death compassed me,
And the straits of the nether-world got hold upon me;
I found trouble and sorrow.
⁴But I called upon the name of the Lord:
'I beseech thee, O Lord, deliver my soul.'
⁵Gracious is the Lord, and righteous;

Yea, our God is compassionate.
⁶The Lord preserveth the simple;
I was brought low, and He saved me.
⁷Return, O my soul, unto Thy rest;
For the Lord hath dealt bountifully with thee.
⁸For thou hast delivered my soul from death,
Mine eyes from tears,
And my feet from stumbling.
⁹I shall walk before the Lord
In the lands of the living.
¹⁰I trusted even when I spoke:
'I am greatly afflicted.'
¹¹I said in my haste:
'All men are liars.'
¹²How can I repay unto the Lord
All His bountiful dealings toward me?
¹³I will lift up the cup of salvation,
And call upon the name of the Lord.
¹⁴My vows will I pay unto the Lord,
Yea, in the presence of all His people.
¹⁵Precious in the sight of the Lord
Is the death of His saints.
¹⁶I beseech Thee, O Lord, for I am Thy servant;
I am Thy servant, the son of Thy handmaid;
Thou hast loosed my bands.
¹⁷I will offer to thee the sacrifice of thanksgiving,
And will call upon the name of the Lord.
¹⁸I will pay my vows unto the Lord,
Yea, in the presence of all His people;
¹⁹In the courts of the Lord's house,
In the midst of thee, O Jerusalem.
Hallelujah.

117O praise the Lord, all ye nations;
Laud Him, all ye peoples.
²For His mercy is great toward us;
And the truth of the Lord endureth for ever.
Hallelujah.

118'O give thanks unto the Lord, for He is good,
For His mercy endureth for ever.
²So let Israel now say,
For His mercy endureth for ever,
³So let the house of Aaron now say,

For His mercy endureth for ever.
⁴So let them now that fear the Lord say,
For His mercy endureth for ever.
⁵Out of my straits I called upon the Lord;
He answered me with great enlargement.
⁶The Lord is for me; I will not fear;
What can man do unto me?
⁷The Lord is for me as my helper;
And I shall gaze upon them that hate me.
⁸It is better to take refuge in the Lord
Than to trust in man.
⁹It is better to take refuge in the Lord
Than to trust in princes.
¹⁰All nations compass me about;
Verily, in the name of the Lord I will cut them off.
¹¹They compass me about, yea, they compass me about;
Verily, in the name of the Lord I will cut them off.
¹²They compass me about like bees;
They are quenched as the fire of thorns;
Verily, in the name of the Lord I will cut them off.
¹³Thou didst thrust sore at me that I might fall;
But the Lord helped me.
¹⁴The Lord is my strength and song;
And He is become my salvation.
¹⁵The voice of rejoicing and salvation is in the tents of the righteous;
The right hand of the Lord doeth valiantly.
¹⁶The right hand of the Lord is exalted;
The right hand of the Lord doeth valiantly.
¹⁷I shall not die, but live,
And declare the works of the Lord.
¹⁸The Lord hath chastened me sore;
But He hath not given me over unto death.
¹⁹Open to me the gates of righteousness;
I will enter into them, I will give thanks unto the Lord.
²⁰This is the gate of the Lord;
The righteous shall enter into it.
²¹I will give thanks unto Thee, for Thou hast answered me,
And art become my salvation.
²²The stone which the builders rejected
Is become the chief corner-stone.
²³This is the Lord's doing;
It is marvellous in our eyes.
²⁴This is the day which the Lord hath made;
We will rejoice and be glad in it.

²⁵We beseech Thee, O Lord, save now!
We beseech Thee, O Lord, make us now to prosper!
²⁶Blessed be he that cometh in the name of the Lord;
We bless you out of the house of the Lord.
²⁷The Lord is God, and hath given us light;
Order the festival procession with boughs, even unto the horns of the altar.
²⁸Thou art my God, and I will give thanks unto Thee;
Thou art my God, I will exalt Thee.
²⁹O give thanks unto the Lord, for He is good,
For His mercy endureth for ever.

119

א ALEPH.
Happy are they that are upright in the way,
Who walk in the law of the Lord.
²Happy are they that keep His testimonies,
That seek Him with the whole heart.
³Yea, they do no unrighteousness;
They walk in His ways.
⁴Thou hast ordained Thy precepts,
That we should observe them diligently.
⁵Oh that my ways were directed
To observe Thy statutes!
⁶Then should I not be ashamed,
When I have regard unto all Thy commandments.
⁷I will give thanks unto Thee with uprightness of heart,
When I learn Thy righteous ordinances.
⁸I will observe Thy statutes;
O forsake me not utterly.
ב BETH.
⁹Wherewithal shall a young man keep his way pure?
By taking heed thereto according to Thy word.
¹⁰With my whole heart have I sought Thee;
O let me not err from Thy commandments.
¹¹Thy word have I laid up in my heart,
That I might not sin against Thee.
¹²Blessed art Thou, O Lord;
Teach me Thy statutes.
¹³With my lips have I told
All the ordinances of Thy mouth.
¹⁴I have rejoiced in the way of Thy testimonies,
As much as in all riches.
¹⁵I will meditate in Thy precepts,
And have respect unto Thy ways.

¹⁶I will delight myself in Thy statutes;
I will not forget Thy word.
ג GIMEL.
¹⁷Deal bountifully with Thy servant that I may live,
And I will observe Thy word.
¹⁸Open Thou mine eyes, that I may behold
Wondrous things out of Thy law.
¹⁹I am a sojourner in the earth;
Hide not Thy commandments from me.
²⁰My soul breaketh for the longing
That it hath unto Thine ordinances at all times.
²¹Thou hast rebuked the proud that are cursed,
That do err from Thy commandments.
²²Take away from me reproach and contempt;
For I have kept Thy testimonies.
²³Even though princes sit and talk against me,
Thy servant doth meditate in Thy statutes.
²⁴Yea, Thy testimonies are my delight,
They are my counsellors.
ד DALETH.
²⁵My soul cleaveth unto the dust;
Quicken Thou me according to Thy word.
²⁶I told of my ways, and Thou didst answer me;
Teach me Thy statutes.
²⁷Make me to understand the way of Thy precepts,
That I may talk of Thy wondrous works.
²⁸My soul melteth away for heaviness;
Sustain me according unto Thy word.
²⁹Remove from me the way of falsehood;
And grant me Thy law graciously.
³⁰I have chosen the way of faithfulness;
Thine ordinances have I set [before me].
³¹I cleave unto Thy testimonies;
O Lord, put me not to shame.
³²I will run the way of Thy commandments,
For Thou dost enlarge my heart.
ה HE.
³³Teach me, O Lord, the way of Thy statutes;
And I will keep it at every step.
³⁴Give me understanding, that I keep Thy law
And observe it with my whole heart.
³⁵Make me to tread in the path of Thy commandments;
For therein do I delight.
³⁶Incline my heart unto Thy testimonies,

And not to covetousness.

[37]Turn away mine eyes from beholding vanity,

And quicken me in Thy ways.

[38]Confirm Thy word unto Thy servant,

Which pertaineth unto the fear of Thee.

[39]Turn away my reproach which I dread;

For Thine ordinances are good.

[40]Behold, I have longed after Thy precepts;

Quicken me in Thy righteousness.

ı VAU.

[41]Let Thy mercies also come unto me, O Lord,

Even Thy salvation, according to Thy word;

[42]That I may have an answer for him that taunteth me;

For I trust in Thy word.

[43]And take not the word of truth utterly out of my mouth;

For I hope in Thine ordinances;

[44]So shall I observe Thy law continually

For ever and ever;

[45]And I will walk at ease,

For I have sought Thy precepts;

[46]I will also speak of Thy testimonies before kings,

And will not be ashamed.

[47]And I will delight myself in Thy commandments,

Which I have loved.

[48]I will lift up my hands also unto Thy commandments, which I have loved;

And I will meditate in Thy statutes.

т ZAIN.

[49]Remember the word unto Thy servant,

Because Thou hast made me to hope.

[50]This is my comfort in my affliction,

That Thy word hath quickened me.

[51]The proud have had me greatly in derision;

Yet have I not turned aside from Thy law.

[52]I have remembered Thine ordinances which are of old, O Lord,

And have comforted myself.

[53]Burning indignation hath taken hold upon me, because of the wicked

That forsake Thy law.

[54]Thy statutes have been my songs

In the house of my pilgrimage.

[55]I have remembered Thy name, O Lord, in the night,

And have observed Thy law.

[56]This I have had,

That I have kept Thy precepts.

n HETH.

[57]My portion is the Lord,
I have said that I would observe Thy words.
[58]I have entreated Thy favour with my whole heart;
Be gracious unto me according to Thy word.
[59]I considered my ways,
And turned my feet unto Thy testimonies.
[60]I made haste, and delayed not,
To observe Thy commandments.
[61]The bands of the wicked have enclosed me;
But I have not forgotten Thy law.
[62]At midnight I will rise to give thanks unto Thee
Because of Thy righteous ordinances.
[63]I am a companion of all them that fear Thee,
And of them that observe Thy precepts.
[64]The earth, O Lord, is full of Thy mercy;
Teach me Thy statutes.
υ TETH.
[65]Thou hast dealt well with Thy servant,
O Lord, according unto Thy word.
[66]Teach me good discernment and knowledge;
For I have believed in Thy commandments.
[67]Before I was afflicted, I did err;
But now I observe Thy word.
[68]Thou art good, and doest good;
Teach me Thy statutes.
[69]The proud have forged a lie against me;
But I with my whole heart will keep Thy precepts.
[70]Their heart is gross like fat;
But I delight in Thy law.
[71]It is good for me that I have been afflicted,
In order that I might learn Thy statutes.
[72]The law of Thy mouth is better unto me
Than thousands of gold and silver.
· IOD.
[73]Thy hands have made me and fashioned me;
Give me understanding, that I may learn Thy commandments.
[74]They that fear Thee shall see me and be glad,
Because I have hope in Thy word.
[75]I know, O Lord, that Thy judgments are righteous,
And that in faithfulness Thou hast afflicted me.
[76]Let, I pray Thee, Thy lovingkindness be ready to comfort me,
According to Thy promise unto Thy servant.
[77]Let Thy tender mercies come unto me, that I may live;
For Thy law is my delight.

[78]Let the proud be put to shame, for they have distorted my cause with falsehood;
But I will meditate in Thy precepts.
[79]Let those that fear Thee return unto me,
And they that know Thy testimonies.
[80]Let my heart be undivided in Thy statutes,
In order that I may not be put to shame.
כ CAPH.
[81]My soul pineth for Thy salvation;
In Thy word do I hope.
[82]Mine eyes fail for Thy word,
Saying: 'When wilt Thou comfort me?'
[83]For I am become like a wine-skin in the smoke;
Yet do I not forget Thy statutes.
[84]How many are the days of Thy servant?
When wilt Thou execute judgment on them that persecute me?
[85]The proud have digged pits for me,
Which is not according to Thy law.
[86]All Thy commandments are faithful;
They persecute me for nought; help Thou me.
[87]They had almost consumed me upon earth;
But as for me, I forsook not Thy precepts.
[88]Quicken me after Thy lovingkindness,
And I will observe the testimony of Thy mouth.
ל LAMED.
[89]For ever, O Lord,
Thy word standeth fast in heaven.
[90]Thy faithfulness is unto all generations;
Thou hast established the earth, and it standeth.
[91]They stand this day according to Thine ordinances;
For all things are Thy servants.
[92]Unless Thy law had been my delight,
I should then have perished in mine affliction.
[93]I will never forget Thy precepts;
For with them Thou hast quickened me.
[94]I am Thine, save me;
For I have sought Thy precepts.
[95]The wicked have waited for me to destroy me;
But I will consider Thy testimonies.
[96]I have seen an end to every purpose;
But Thy commandment is exceeding broad.
מ MEM.
[97]O how love I Thy law!
It is my meditation all the day.
[98]Thy commandments make me wiser than mine enemies:

For they are ever with me.

[99]I have more understanding than all my teachers;

For Thy testimonies are my meditation.

[100]I understand more than mine elders,

Because I have keep Thy precepts.

[101]I have refrained my feet from every evil way,

In order that I might observe Thy word.

[102]I have not turned aside from Thine ordinances;

For Thou hast instructed me.

[103]How sweet are Thy words unto my palate!

Yea, sweeter than honey to my mouth!

[104]From Thy precepts I get understanding;

Therefore I hate every false way.

ב NUN.

[105]Thy word is a lamp unto my feet,

And a light unto my path.

[106]I have sworn, and have confirmed it,

To observe Thy righteous ordinances.

[107]I am afflicted very much;

Quicken me, O Lord, according unto Thy word.

[108]Accept, I beseech Thee, the freewill-offerings of my mouth, O Lord,

And teach me Thine ordinances.

[109]My soul is continually in my hand;

Yet have I not forgotten Thy law.

[110]The wicked have laid a snare for me;

Yet went I not astray from Thy precepts.

[111]Thy testimonies have I taken as a heritage for ever;

For they are the rejoicing of my heart.

[112]I have inclined my heart to perform Thy statutes,

For ever, at every step.

ס SAMECH.

[113]I hate them that are of a double mind;

But Thy law do I love.

[114]Thou art my covert and my shield;

In Thy word do I hope.

[115]Depart from me, ye evil-doers;

That I may keep the commandments of my God.

[116]Uphold me according unto Thy word, that I may live;

And put me not to shame in my hope.

[117]Support Thou me, and I shall be saved;

And I will occupy myself with Thy statutes continually.

[118]Thou hast made light of all them that err from Thy statutes;

For their deceit is vain.

[119]Thou puttest away all the wicked of the earth like dross;

Therefore I love Thy testimonies.
[120]My flesh shuddereth for fear of Thee;
And I am afraid of Thy judgments.

ע AIN.
[121]I have done justice and righteousness;
Leave me not to mine oppressors.
[122]Be surety for Thy servant for good;
Let not the proud oppress me.
[123]Mine eyes fail for Thy salvation,
And for Thy righteous word.
[124]Deal with Thy servant according unto Thy mercy,
And teach me Thy statutes.
[125]I am Thy servant, give me understanding,
That I may know Thy testimonies.
[126]It is time for the Lord to work;
They have made void Thy law.
[127]Therefore I love Thy commandments
Above gold, yea, above fine gold.
[128]Therefore I esteem all [Thy] precepts concerning all things to be right;
Every false way I hate.

פ PE.
[129]Thy testimonies are wonderful;
Therefore doth my soul keep them.
[130]The opening of Thy words giveth light;
It giveth understanding unto the simple.
[131]I opened wide my mouth, and panted;
For I longed for Thy commandments.
[132]Turn Thee towards me, and be gracious unto me,
As is Thy wont to do unto those that love Thy name.
[133]Order my footsteps by Thy word;
And let not any iniquity have dominion over me.
[134]Redeem me from the oppression of man,
And I will observe Thy precepts.
[135]Make Thy face to shine upon Thy servant;
And teach me Thy statutes.
[136]Mine eyes run down with rivers of water,
Because they observe not Thy law.

צ TZADE.
[137]Righteous art Thou, O Lord,
And upright are Thy judgments.
[138]Thou hast commanded Thy testimonies in righteousness
And exceeding faithfulness.
[139]My zeal hath undone me,
Because mine adversaries have forgotten Thy words.

¹⁴⁰Thy word is tried to the uttermost,
And Thy servant loveth it.
¹⁴¹I am small and despised;
Yet have I not forgotten Thy precepts.
¹⁴²Thy righteousness is an everlasting righteousness,
And Thy law is truth.
¹⁴³Trouble and anguish have overtaken me;
Yet Thy commandments are my delight.
¹⁴⁴Thy testimonies are righteous for ever;
Give me understanding, and I shall live.
ק KOPH.
¹⁴⁵I have called with my whole heart; answer me, O Lord;
I will keep Thy statutes.
¹⁴⁶I have called Thee, save me,
And I will observe Thy testimonies.
¹⁴⁷I rose early at dawn, and cried;
I hoped in Thy word.
¹⁴⁸Mine eyes forestalled the nightwatches,
That I might meditate in Thy word.
¹⁴⁹Hear my voice according unto Thy lovingkindness;
Quicken me, O Lord, as Thou art wont.
¹⁵⁰They draw nigh that follow after wickedness;
They are far from Thy law.
¹⁵¹Thou art nigh, O Lord;
And all Thy commandments are truth.
¹⁵²Of old have I known from Thy testimonies
That Thou hast founded them for ever.

ר RESH.
¹⁵³O see mine affliction, and rescue me;
For I do not forget Thy law.
¹⁵⁴Plead Thou my cause, and redeem me;
Quicken me according to Thy word.
¹⁵⁵Salvation is far from the wicked;
For they seek not Thy statutes.
¹⁵⁶Great are Thy compassions, O Lord;
Quicken me as Thou art wont.
¹⁵⁷Many are my persecutors and mine adversaries;
Yet have I not turned aside from Thy testimonies.
¹⁵⁸I beheld them that were faithless, and strove with them;
Because they observed not Thy word.
¹⁵⁹O see how I love Thy precepts;
Quicken me, O Lord, according to Thy lovingkindness.
¹⁶⁰The beginning of Thy word is truth;

And all Thy righteous ordinance endureth for ever.

ש SHIN.
161Princes have persecuted me without a cause;
But my heart standeth in awe of Thy words.
162I rejoice at Thy word,
As one that findeth great spoil.
163I hate and abhor falsehood;
Thy law do I love.
164Seven times a day do I praise Thee,
Because of Thy righteous ordinances.
165Great peace have they that love Thy law;
And there is no stumbling for them.
166I have hoped for Thy salvation, O Lord,
And have done Thy commandments.
167My soul hath observed Thy testimonies;
And I love them exceedingly.
168I have observed Thy precepts and Thy testimonies;
For all my ways are before Thee.

ת TAU.
169Let my cry come near before Thee, O Lord;
Give me understanding according to Thy word.
170Let my supplication come before Thee;
Deliver me according to Thy word.
171Let my lips utter praise:
Because Thou teachest me Thy statutes.
172Let my tongue sing of Thy word;
For all Thy commandments are righteousness.
173Let Thy hand be ready to help me;
For I have chosen Thy precepts.
174I have longed for Thy salvation, O Lord;
And Thy law is my delight.
175Let my soul live, and it shall praise Thee;
And let Thine ordinances help me.
176I have gone astray like a lost sheep; seek Thy servant;
For I have not forgotten Thy commandments.

120A Song of Ascents.
In my distress I called unto the Lord,
And He answered me.
2O Lord, deliver my soul from lying lips,
From a deceitful tongue.
3What shall be given unto thee, and what shall be done more unto thee,

Thou deceitful tongue?
⁴Sharp arrows of the mighty,
With coals of broom.
⁵Woe is me, that I sojourn with Meshech,
That I dwell beside the tents of Kedar!
⁶My soul hath full long had her dwelling
With him that hateth peace.
⁷I am all peace;
But when I speak, they are for war.

121A Song of Ascents.
I will lift up mine eyes unto the mountains:
From whence shall my help come?
²My help cometh from the Lord,
Who made heaven and earth.
³He will not suffer thy foot to be moved;
He that keepeth thee will not slumber.
⁴Behold, He that keepeth Israel
Doth neither slumber nor sleep.
⁵The Lord is thy keeper;
The Lord is thy shade upon thy right hand.
⁶The sun shall not smite thee by day,
Nor the moon by night.
⁷The Lord shall keep thee from all evil;
He shall keep thy soul.
⁸The Lord shall guard thy going out and thy coming in,
From this time forth and for ever.

122A Song of Ascents; of David.

I rejoiced when they said unto me:
'Let us go unto the house of the Lord.'
²Our feet are standing
Within thy gates, O Jerusalem;
³Jerusalem, that art builded
As a city that is compact together;
⁴Whither the tribes went up, even the tribes of the Lord,
As a testimony unto Israel,
To give thanks unto the name of the Lord.
⁵For there were set thrones for judgment,
The thrones of the house of David.
⁶Pray for the peace of Jerusalem;
May they prosper that love thee.
⁷Peace be within thy walls,

And prosperity within thy palaces.
⁸For my brethren and companions' sakes,
I will now say: 'Peace be within thee.'
⁹For the sake of the house of the Lord our God
I will seek thy good.

123A Song of Ascents.
Unto Thee I lift up mine eyes,
O Thou that art enthroned in the heavens.
²Behold, as the eyes of servants unto the hand of their master,
As the eyes of a maiden unto the hand of her mistress;
So our eyes look unto the Lord our God,
Until He be gracious unto us.
³Be gracious unto us, O Lord, be gracious unto us;
For we are full sated with contempt.
⁴Our soul is full sated
With the scorning of those that are at ease,
And with the contempt of the proud oppressors.

124A Song of Ascents; of David.
'If it had not been the Lord who was for us',
Let Israel now say;
²'If it had not been the Lord who was for us,
When men rose up against us,
³Then they had swallowed us up alive,
When their wrath was kindled against us;
⁴Then the waters had overwhelmed us,
The stream had gone over our soul;
⁵Then the proud waters
Had gone over our soul.'
⁶Blessed be the Lord,
Wo hath not given us as a prey to their teeth.
⁷Our soul is escaped as a bird out of the snare of the fowlers;
The snare is broken, and we are escaped.
⁸Our help is in the name of the Lord,
Who made heaven and earth.

125A Song of Ascents.
They that trust in the Lord
Are as mount Zion, which cannot be moved, but abideth for ever.
²As the mountains are round about Jerusalem,
So the Lord is round about His people,
From this time forth and for ever.
³For the rod of wickedness shall not rest upon the lot of the righteous;

That the righteous put not forth their hands unto iniquity.
⁴Do good, O Lord, unto the good,
And to them that are upright in their hearts.
⁵But as for such as turn aside unto their crooked ways,
The Lord will lead them away with the workers of iniquity.
Peace be upon Israel.

126A Song of Ascents.
When the Lord brought back those that returned to Zion,
We were like unto them that dream.
²Then was our mouth filled with laughter,
And our tongue with singing;
Then said they among the nations:
'The Lord hath done great things with these.'
³The Lord hath done great things with us;
We are rejoiced.
⁴Turn our captivity, O Lord,
As the streams in the dry land.
⁵They that sow in tears
Shall reap in joy.
⁶Though he goeth on his way weeping that beareth the measure of seed,
He shall come home with joy, bearing his sheaves.

127A Song of Ascents; of Solomon.
Except the Lord build the house,
They labour in vain that build it;
Except the Lord keep the city,
The watchman waketh but in vain.
²It is vain for you that ye rise early, and sit up late,
Ye that eat the bread of toil;
So He giveth unto His beloved in sleep.
³Lo, children are a heritage of the Lord;
The fruit of the womb is a reward.
⁴As arrows in the hand of a mighty man,
So are the children of one's youth.
⁵Happy is the man that hath his quiver full of them;
They shall not be put to shame,
When they speak with their enemies in the gate.

128A Song of Ascents.
Happy is every one that feareth the Lord,
That walketh in His ways.
²When thou eatest the labour of thy hands,
Happy shalt thou be, and it shall be well with thee.

³Thy wife shall be as a fruitful vine, in the innermost parts of thy house;
Thy children like olive plants, round about thy table.
⁴Behold, surely thus shall the man be blessed
That feareth the Lord.
⁵The Lord bless thee out of Zion;
And see thou the good of Jerusalem all the days of thy life;
⁶And see thy children's children.
Peace be upon Israel!

129A Song of Ascents.
'Much have they afflicted me from my youth up',
Let Israel now say;
²'Much have they afflicted me from my youth up;
But they have not prevailed against me.
³The plowers plowed upon my back;
They made long their furrows.
⁴The Lord is righteous;
He hath cut asunder the cords of the wicked.'
⁵Let them be ashamed and turned backward,
All they that hate Zion.
⁶Let them be as the grass upon the housetops,
Which withereth afore it springeth up;
⁷Wherewith the reaper filleth not his hand,
Nor he that bindeth sheaves his bosom.
⁸Neither do they that go by say:
'The blessing of the Lord be upon you;
We bless you in the name of the Lord.'

130A Song of Ascents.
Out of the depths have I called Thee, O Lord.
²Lord, hearken unto my voice;
Let Thine ears be attentive
To the voice of my supplications.
³If Thou, Lord, shouldest mark iniquities,
O Lord, who could stand?
⁴For with Thee there is forgiveness,
That Thou mayest be feared.
⁵I wait for the Lord, my soul doth wait,
And in His word do I hope.
⁶My soul waiteth for the Lord,
More than watchmen for the morning;
Yea, more than watchmen for the morning.
⁷O Israel, hope in the Lord;
For with the Lord there is mercy,

And with Him is plenteous redemption.
[8]And He will redeem Israel
From all his iniquities.

131A Song of Ascents; of David.
Lord, my heart is not haughty, nor mine eyes lofty;
Neither do I exercise myself in things too great, or in things too wonderful for me.
[2]Surely I have stilled and quieted my soul;
Like a weaned child with his mother;
My soul is with me like a weaned child.
[3]O Israel, hope in the Lord
From this time forth and for ever.

132A Song of Ascents.
Lord, remember unto David
All his affliction;
[2]How he swore unto the Lord,
And vowed unto the Mighty One of Jacob:
[3]'Surely I will not come into the tent of my house,
Nor go up into the bed that is spread for me;
[4]I will not give sleep to mine eyes,
Nor slumber to mine eyelids;
[5]Until I find out a place for the Lord,
A dwelling-place for the Mighty One of Jacob.'
[6]Lo, we heard of it as being in Ephrath;
We found it in the field of [5]the wood.
[7]Let us go into His dwelling-place;
Let us worship at His footstool.
[8]Arise, O Lord, unto Thy resting-place;
Thou, and the ark of Thy strength.
[9]Let Thy priests be clothed with righteousness;
And let Thy saints shout for joy.
[10]For Thy servant David's sake
Turn not away the face of Thine anointed.
[11]The Lord swore unto David in truth;
He will not turn back from it:
'Of the fruit of thy body will I set upon thy throne.
[12]If thy children keep My covenant
And My testimony that I shall teach them,
Their children also for ever shall sit upon thy throne.'
[13]For the Lord hath chosen Zion;
He hath desired it for His habitation:
[14]'This is My resting-place for ever;
Here will I dwell; for I have desired it.

¹⁵I will abundantly bless her provision;
I will give her needy bread in plenty.
¹⁶Her priests also will I clothe with salvation;
And her saints shall shout aloud for joy.
¹⁷There will I make a horn to shoot up unto David,
There have I ordered a lamp for Mine anointed.
¹⁸His enemies will I clothe with shame;
But upon himself shall his crown shine.'

133A Song of Ascents; of David.
Behold, how good and how pleasant it is
For brethren to dwell together in unity!
²It is like the precious oil upon the head,
Coming down upon the beard;
Even Aaron's beard,
That cometh down upon the collar of his garments;
³Like the dew of Hermon,
That cometh down upon the mountains of Zion;
For there the Lord commanded the blessing,
Even life for ever.

134A Song of Ascents.
Behold, bless ye the Lord, all ye servants of the Lord,
That stand in the house of the Lord in the night seasons.
²Lift up your hands to the sanctuary,
And bless ye the Lord.
³The Lord bless thee out of Zion;
Even He that made heaven and earth.

135Hallelujah.
Praise ye the name of the Lord;
Give praise, O ye servants of the Lord,
²Ye that stand in the house of the Lord,
In the courts of the house of our God.
³Praise ye the Lord, for the Lord is good;
Sing praises unto His name, for it is pleasant.
⁴For the Lord hath chosen Jacob unto Himself,
And Israel for His own treasure.
⁵For I know that the Lord is great,
And that our Lord is above all gods.
⁶Whatsoever the Lord pleased, that hath He done,
In heaven and in earth, in the seas and in all deeps;
⁷Who causeth the vapours to ascend from the ends of the earth;
He maketh lightnings for the rain;

He bringeth forth the wind out of His treasuries.
[8]Who smote the first-born of Egypt,
Both of man and beast.
[9]He sent signs and wonders into the midst of thee, O Egypt,
Upon Pharaoh, and upon all his servants.
[10]Who smote many nations,
And slew mighty kings:
[11]Sihon king of the Amorites,
And Og king of Bashan,
And all the kingdoms of Canaan;
[12]And gave their land for a heritage,
A heritage unto Israel His people.
[13]O Lord, Thy name endureth for ever;
Thy memorial, O Lord, throughout all generations.
[14]For the Lord will judge His people,
And repent Himself for His servants.
[15]The idols of the nations are silver and gold,
The work of men's hands.
[16]They have mouths, but they speak not;
Eyes have they, but they see not;
[17]They have ears, but they hear not;
Neither is there any breath in their mouths.
[18]They that make them shall be like unto them;
Yea, every one that trusteth in them.
[19]O house of Israel, bless ye the Lord;
O house of Aaron, bless ye the Lord;
[20]O house of Levi, bless ye the Lord;
Ye that fear the Lord, bless ye the Lord.
[21]Blessed be the Lord out of Zion,
Who dwelleth at Jerusalem.
Hallelujah.

136O give thanks unto the Lord, for He is good,
For His mercy endureth for ever.
[2]O give thanks unto the God of gods,
For His mercy endureth for ever.
[3]O give thanks unto the Lord of lords,
For His mercy endureth for ever.
[4]To Him who alone doeth great wonders,
For His mercy endureth for ever.
[5]To Him that by understanding made the heavens,
For His mercy endureth for ever.
[6]To Him that spread forth the earth above the waters,
For His mercy endureth for ever.

⁷To Him that made great lights,
For His mercy endureth for ever;
⁸The sun to rule by day,
For His mercy endureth for ever;
⁹The moon and stars to rule by night,
For His mercy endureth for ever.
¹⁰To Him that smote Egypt in their first-born,
For His mercy endureth for ever;
¹¹And brought out Israel from among them,
For His mercy endureth for ever;
¹²With a strong hand, and with an outstretched arm,
For His mercy endureth for ever.
¹³To Him who divided the Red Sea in sunder,
For His mercy endureth for ever;
¹⁴And made Israel to pass through the midst of it,
For His mercy endureth for ever;
¹⁵But overthrew Pharaoh and his host in the Red Sea,
For His mercy endureth for ever.
¹⁶To Him that led His people through the wilderness,
For His mercy endureth for ever.
¹⁷To Him that smote great kings;
For His mercy endureth for ever;
¹⁸And slew mighty kings,
For His mercy endureth for ever.
¹⁹Sihon king of the Amorites,
For His mercy endureth for ever;
²⁰And Og king of Bashan,
For His mercy endureth for ever;
²¹And gave their land for a heritage,
For His mercy endureth for ever;
²²Even a heritage unto Israel His servant,
For His mercy endureth for ever.
²³Who remembered us in our low estate,
For His mercy endureth for ever;
²⁴And hath delivered us from our adversaries,
For His mercy endureth for ever.
²⁵Who giveth food to all flesh,
For His mercy endureth for ever.
²⁶O give thanks unto the God of heaven,
For His mercy endureth for ever.

137By the rivers of Babylon,
There we sat down, yea, we wept,
When we remembered Zion.

²Upon the willows in the midst thereof
We hanged up our harps.
³For there they that led us captive asked of us words of song,
And our tormentors asked of us mirth:
'Sing us one of the songs of Zion.'
⁴How shall we sing the Lord's song
In a foreign land?
⁵If I forget thee, O Jerusalem,
Let my right hand forget her cunning.
⁶Let my tongue cleave to the roof of my mouth,
If I remember thee not;
If I set not Jerusalem
Above my chiefest joy.
⁷Remember, O Lord, against the children of Edom
The day of Jerusalem;
Who said: 'Rase it, rase it,
Even to the foundation thereof.'
⁸O daughter of Babylon, that art to be destroyed;
Happy shall he be, that repayeth thee
As thou hast served us.
⁹Happy shall he be, that taketh and dasheth thy little ones
Against the rock.

138[A Psalm] of David.
I will give Thee thanks with my whole heart,
In the presence of the mighty will I sing praises unto Thee.
²I will bow down toward Thy holy temple,
And give thanks unto Thy name for Thy mercy and for Thy truth;
For Thou hast magnified Thy word above all Thy name.
³In the day that I called, Thou didst answer me;
Thou didst encourage me in my soul with strength.
⁴All the kings of the earth shall give Thee thanks, O Lord,
For they have heard the words of Thy mouth.
⁵Yea, they shall sing of the ways of the Lord;
For great is the glory of the Lord.
⁶For though the Lord be high, yet regardeth He the lowly,
And the haughty He knoweth from afar.
⁷Though I walk in the midst of trouble, Thou quickenest me;
Thou stretchest forth Thy hand against the wrath of mine enemies,
And Thy right hand doth save me.
⁸The Lord will accomplish that which concerneth me;
Thy mercy, O Lord, endureth for ever;
Forsake not the work of Thine own hands.

139For the Leader. A Psalm of David.
O Lord, Thou hast searched me, and known me.
²Thou knowest my downsitting and mine uprising,
Thou understandest my thought afar off.
³Thou measurest my going about and my lying down,
And art acquainted with all my ways.
⁴For there is not a word in my tongue,
But, lo, O Lord, Thou knowest it altogether.
⁵Thou hast hemmed me in behind and before,
And laid Thy hand upon me.
⁶Such knowledge is too wonderful for me;
Too high, I cannot attain unto it.
⁷Whither shall I go from Thy spirit?
Or whither shall I flee from Thy presence?
⁸If I ascend up into heaven, Thou art there;
If I make my bed in the nether-world, behold, Thou art there.
⁹If I take the wings of the morning,
And dwell in the uttermost parts of the sea;
¹⁰Even there would Thy hand lead me,
And Thy right hand would hold me.
¹¹And if I say: 'Surely the darkness shall envelop me,
And the light about me shall be night';
¹²Even the darkness is not too dark for Thee,
But the night shineth as the day;
The darkness is even as the light.
¹³For Thou hast made my reins;
Thou hast knit me together in my mother's womb.
¹⁴I will give thanks unto Thee, for I am fearfully and wonderfully made;
Wonderful are Thy works; and that my soul knoweth right well.
¹⁵My frame was not hidden from Thee,
When I was made in secret,
And curiously wrought in the lowest parts of the earth.
¹⁶Thine eyes did see mine unformed substance,
And in Thy book they were all written—
Even the days that were fashioned,
When as yet there was none of them.
¹⁷How weighty also are Thy thoughts unto me, O God!
How great is the sum of them!
¹⁸If I would count them, they are more in number than the sand;
Were I to come to the end of them, I would still be with Thee.
¹⁹If Thou but wouldest slay the wicked, O God—
Depart from me therefore, ye men of blood;
²⁰Who utter Thy name with wicked thought,
They take it for falsehood, even Thine enemies—

^{21}Do not I hate them, O Lord, that hate Thee?
And do not I strive with those that rise up against Thee?
^{22}I hate them with utmost hatred;
I count them mine enemies.
^{23}Search me, O God, and know my heart,
Try me, and know my thoughts;
^{24}And see if there be any way in me that is grievous,
And lead me in the way everlasting.

140For the Leader. A Psalm of David.
^{2}Deliver me, O Lord, from the evil man;
Preserve me from the violent man;
^{3}Who devise evil things in their heart;
Every day do they stir up wars.
^{4}They have sharpened their tongue like a serpent;
Vipers' venom is under their lips.Selah
^{5}Keep me, O Lord, from the hands of the wicked;
Preserve me from the violent man;
Who have purposed to make my steps slip.
^{6}The proud have hid a snare for me, and cords;
They have spread a net by the wayside;
They have set gins for me.Selah
^{7}I have said unto the Lord: 'Thou art my God';
Give ear, O Lord, unto the voice of my supplications.
^{8}O God the Lord, the strength of my salvation,
Who hast screened my head in the day of battle,
^{9}Grant not, O Lord, the desires of the wicked;
Further not his evil device, so that they exalt themselves.Selah
^{10}As for the head of those that compass me about,
Let the mischief of their own lips cover them.
^{11}Let burning coals fall upon them;
Let them be cast into the fire,
Into deep pits, that they rise not up again.
^{12}A slanderer shall not be established in the earth;
The violent and evil man shall be hunted with thrust upon thrust.
^{13}I know that the Lord will maintain the cause of the poor,
And the right of the needy.
^{14}Surely the righteous shall give thanks unto Thy name;
The upright shall dwell in Thy presence.

141A Psalm of David.
Lord, I have called Thee; make haste unto me;
Give ear unto my voice, when I call unto Thee.
^{2}Let my prayer be set forth as incense before Thee,

The lifting up of my hands as the evening sacrifice.
³Set a guard, O Lord, to my mouth;
Keep watch at the door of my lips.
⁴Incline not my heart to any evil thing,
To be occupied in deeds of wickedness
With men that work iniquity;
And let me not eat of their dainties.
⁵Let the righteous smite me in kindness, and correct me;
Oil so choice let not my head refuse;
For still is my prayer because of their wickedness.
⁶Their judges are thrown down by the sides of the rock;
And they shall hear my words, that they are sweet.
⁷As when one cleaveth and breaketh up the earth,
Our bones are scattered at the grave's mouth.
⁸For mine eyes are unto Thee, O God the Lord;
In Thee have I taken refuge, O pour not out my soul.
⁹Keep me from the snare which they have laid for me,
And from the gins of the workers of iniquity.
¹⁰Let the wicked fall into their own nets,
Whilst I withal escape.

142Maschil of David, when he was in the cave; a Prayer.
²With my voice I cry unto the Lord;
With my voice I make supplication unto the Lord.
³I pour out my complaint before Him,
I declare before Him my trouble;
⁴When my spirit fainteth within me—
Thou knowest my path—
In the way wherein I walk
Have they hidden a snare for me.
⁵Look on my right hand, and see,
For there is no man that knoweth me;
I have no way to flee;
No man careth for my soul.
⁶I have cried unto Thee, O Lord;
I have said: 'Thou art my refuge,
My portion in the land of the living.'
⁷Attend unto my cry;
For I am brought very low;
Deliver me from my persecutors;
For they are too strong for me.
⁸Bring my soul out of prison,
That I may give thanks unto Thy name;
The righteous shall crown themselves because of me;

For Thou wilt deal bountifully with me.

143A Psalm of David.
O Lord, hear my prayer, give ear to my supplications;
In Thy faithfulness answer me, and in Thy righteousness.
[2]And enter not into judgment with Thy servant;
For in Thy sight shall no man living be justified.
[3]For the enemy hath persecuted my soul;
He hath crushed my life down to the ground;
He hath made me to dwell in darkness, as those that have been long dead.
[4]And my spirit fainteth within me;
My heart within me is appalled.
[5]I remember the days of old;
I meditate on all Thy doing;
I muse on the work of Thy hands.
[6]I spread forth my hands unto Thee;
My soul [thirsteth] after Thee, as a weary land. Selah
[7]Answer me speedily, O Lord,
My spirit faileth;
Hide not Thy face from me;
Lest I become like them that go down into the pit.
[8]Cause me to hear Thy lovingkindness in the morning,
For in Thee do I trust;
Cause me to know the way wherein I should walk,
For unto Thee have I lifted up my soul.
[9]Deliver me from mine enemies, O Lord;
With Thee have I hidden myself.
[10]Teach me to do Thy will,
For Thou art my God;
Let Thy good spirit
Lead me in an even land.
[11]For Thy name's sake, O Lord, quicken me;
In Thy righteousness bring my soul out of trouble.
[12]And in Thy mercy cut off mine enemies,
And destroy all them that harass my soul;
For I am Thy servant.

144[A Psalm] of David.
Blessed be the Lord my Rock,
Who traineth my hands for war,
And my fingers for battle;
[2]My lovingkindness, and my fortress,
My high tower, and my deliverer;
My shield, and He in whom I take refuge;

Who subdueth my people under me.
3Lord, what is man, that Thou takest knowledge of him?
Or the son of man, that Thou makest account of him?
4Man is like unto a breath;
His days are as a shadow that passeth away.
5O Lord, bow Thy heavens, and come down;
Touch the mountains, that they may smoke.
6Cast forth lightning, and scatter them;
Send out Thine arrows, and discomfit them.
7Stretch forth Thy hands from on high;
Rescue me, and deliver me out of many waters,
Out of the hand of strangers;
8Whose mouth speaketh falsehood,
And their right hand is a right hand of lying.
9O God, I will sing a new song unto Thee,
Upon a psaltery of ten strings will I sing praises unto Thee;
10Who givest salvation unto kings,
Who rescuest David Thy servant from the hurtful sword.
11Rescue me, and deliver me out of the hand of strangers,
Whose mouth speaketh falsehood,
And their right hand is a right hand of lying.
12We whose sons are as plants grown up in their youth;
Whose daughters are as corner-pillars carved after the fashion of a palace;
13Whose garners are full, affording all manner of store;
Whose sheep increase by thousands and ten thousands in our fields;
14Whose oxen are well laden;
With no breach, and no going forth,
And no outcry in our broad places;
15Happy is the people that is in such a case.
Yea, happy is the people whose God is the Lord.

145[A Psalm of] praise; of David.
אI will extol Thee, my God, O King;
And I will bless Thy for name ever and ever.
2בEvery day will I bless Thee;
And I will praise Thy name for ever and ever.
3גGreat is the Lord, and highly to be praised;
And His greatness is unsearchable.
4דOne generation shall laud Thy works to another,
And shall declare Thy mighty acts.
5הThe glorious splendour of Thy majesty,
And Thy wondrous works, will I rehearse.
6ןAnd men shall speak of the might of Thy tremendous acts;
And I will tell of Thy greatness.

[7]רThey shall utter the fame of Thy great goodness,
And shall sing of Thy righteousness.
[8]נThe Lord is gracious, and full of compassion;
Slow to anger, and of great mercy.
[9]טThe Lord is good to all;
And His tender mercies are over all His works.
[10]יAll Thy works shall praise Thee, O Lord;
And Thy saints shall bless Thee.
[11]כThey shall speak of the glory of Thy kingdom,
And talk of Thy might;
[12]לTo make known to the sons of men His mighty acts,
And the glory of the majesty of His kingdom.
[13]מThy kingdom is a kingdom for all ages,
And Thy dominion endureth throughout all generations.
[14]סThe Lord upholdeth all that fall,
And raiseth up all those that are bowed down.
[15]עThe eyes of all wait for Thee,
And Thou givest them their food in due season.
[16]פThou openest Thy hand,
And satisfiest every living thing with favour.
[17]צThe Lord is righteous in all His ways,
And gracious in all His works.
[18]קThe Lord is nigh unto all them that call upon Him,
To all that call upon Him in truth.
[19]רHe will fulfil the desire of them that fear Him;
He also will hear their cry, and will save them.
[20]שThe Lord preserveth all them that love Him;
But all the wicked will He destroy.
[21]תMy mouth shall speak the praise of the Lord;
And let all flesh bless His holy name for ever and ever.

146Hallelujah.
Praise the Lord, O my soul.
[2]I will praise the Lord while I live;
I will sing praises unto my God while I have my being.
[3]Put not your trust in princes,
Nor in the son of man, in whom there is no help.
[4]His breath goeth forth, he returneth to his dust;
In that very day his thoughts perish.
[5]Happy is he whose help is the God of Jacob,
Whose hope is in the Lord his God,
[6]Who made heaven and earth,
The sea, and all that in them is;
Who keepeth truth for ever;

⁷Who executeth justice for the oppressed;
Who giveth bread to the hungry.
The Lord looseth the prisoners;
⁸The Lord openeth the eyes of the blind;
The Lord raiseth up them that are bowed down;
The Lord loveth the righteous;
⁹The Lord preserveth the strangers;
He upholdeth the fatherless and the widow;
But the way of the wicked He maketh crooked.
¹⁰The Lord will reign for ever,
Thy God, O Zion, unto all generations.
Hallelujah.

147Hallelujah;
For it is good to sing praises unto our God;
For it is pleasant, and praise is comely.
²The Lord doth build up Jerusalem,
He gathereth together the dispersed of Israel;
³Who healeth the broken in heart,
And bindeth up their wounds.
⁴He counteth the number of the stars;
He giveth them all their names.
⁵Great is our Lord, and mighty in power;
His understanding is infinite.
⁶The Lord upholdeth the humble;
He bringeth the wicked down to the ground.
⁷Sing unto the Lord with thanksgiving,
Sing praises upon the harp unto our God;
⁸Who covereth the heaven with clouds,
Who prepareth rain for the earth,
Who maketh the mountains to spring with grass.
⁹He giveth to the beast his food,
And to the young ravens which cry.
¹⁰He delighteth not in the strength of the horse;
He taketh no pleasure in the legs of a man.
¹¹The Lord taketh pleasure in them that fear Him,
In those that wait for His mercy.
¹²Glorify the Lord, O Jerusalem;
Praise thy God, O Zion.
¹³For He hath made strong the bars of thy gates;
He hath blessed thy children within thee.
¹⁴He maketh thy borders peace;
He giveth thee in plenty the fat of wheat.
¹⁵He sendeth out His commandment upon earth;

His word runneth very swiftly.
¹⁶He giveth snow like wool;
He scattereth the hoar-frost like ashes.
¹⁷He casteth forth His ice like crumbs;
Who can stand before His cold?
¹⁸He sendeth forth His word, and melteth them;
He causeth His wind to blow, and the waters flow.
¹⁹He declareth His word unto Jacob,
His statutes and His ordinances unto Israel.
²⁰He hath not dealt so with any nation;
And as for His ordinances, they have not known them.
Hallelujah.

148Hallelujah.
Praise ye the Lord from the heavens;
Praise Him in the heights.
²Praise ye Him, all His angels;
Praise ye Him, all His hosts.
³Praise ye Him, sun and moon;
Praise Him, all ye stars of light.
⁴Praise Him, ye heavens of heavens,
And ye waters that are above the heavens.
⁵Let them praise the name of the Lord;
For He commanded, and they were created.
⁶He hath also established them for ever and ever;
He hath made a decree which shall not be transgressed.
⁷Praise the Lord from the earth,
Ye sea-monsters, and all deeps;
⁸Fire and hail, snow and vapour,
Stormy wind, fulfilling His word;
⁹Mountains and all hills,
Fruitful trees and all cedars;
¹⁰Beasts and all cattle,
Creeping things and winged fowl;
¹¹Kings of the earth and all peoples,
Princes and all judges of the earth;
¹²Both young men and maidens,
Old men and children;
¹³Let them praise the name of the Lord,
For His name alone is exalted;
His glory is above the earth and heaven.
¹⁴And He hath lifted up a horn for His people,
A praise for all His saints,
Even for the children of Israel, a people near unto Him.

Hallelujah.

149Hallelujah.
Sing unto the Lord a new song,
And His praise in the assembly of the saints.
2Let Israel rejoice in his Maker;
Let the children of Zion be joyful in their King.
3Let them praise His name in the dance;
Let them sing praises unto Him with the timbrel and harp.
4For the Lord taketh pleasure in His people;
He adorneth the humble with salvation.
5Let the saints exult in glory;
Let them sing for joy upon their beds.
6Let the high praises of God be in their mouth,
And a two-edged sword in their hand;
7To execute vengeance upon the nations,
And chastisements upon the peoples;
8To bind their kings with chains,
And their nobles with fetters of iron;
9To execute upon them the judgment written;
He is the glory of all His saints.
Hallelujah.

150Hallelujah.
Praise God in His sanctuary;
Praise Him in the firmament of His power.
2Praise Him for His mighty acts;
Praise Him according to His abundant greatness.
3Praise Him with the blast of the horn;
Praise Him with the psaltery and harp.
4Praise Him with the timbrel and dance;
Praise Him with stringed instruments and the pipe.
5Praise Him with the loud-sounding cymbals;
Praise Him with the clanging cymbals.
6Let every thing that hath breath praise the Lord.
Hallelujah.

משלי

PROVERBS

1 The proverbs of Solomon the

son of David, king of Israel,

²To know wisdom and instruction;

To comprehend the words of understanding;

³To receive the discipline of wisdom,

Justice, and right, and equity;

⁴To give prudence to the simple,

To the young man knowledge and discretion;

⁵That the wise man may hear, and increase in learning,

And the man of understanding may attain unto wise counsels;

⁶To understand a proverb, and a figure;

The words of the wise, and their dark sayings.

⁷The fear of the Lord is the beginning of knowledge;

But the foolish despise wisdom and discipline.

⁸Hear, my son, the instruction of thy father,

And forsake not the teaching of thy mother;

⁹For they shall be a chaplet of grace unto thy head,

And chains about thy neck.

¹⁰My son, if sinners entice thee,

Consent thou not.

¹¹If they say: 'Come with us,

Let us lie in wait for blood,

Let us lurk for the innocent without cause;

¹²Let us swallow them up alive as the grave,

And whole, as those that go down into the pit;

¹³We shall find all precious substance,

We shall fill our houses with spoil;

¹⁴Cast in thy lot among us;

Let us all have one purse'—

¹⁵My son, walk not thou in the way with them,

Restrain thy foot from their path;

¹⁶For their feet run to evil,

And they make haste to shed blood.

¹⁷For in vain the net is spread

In the eyes of any bird;

¹⁸And these lie in wait for their own blood,

They lurk for their own lives.

¹⁹So are the ways of every one that is greedy of gain;

It taketh away the life of the owners thereof.

²⁰Wisdom crieth aloud in the street,

She uttereth her voice in the broad places;

²¹She calleth at the head of the noisy streets,

At the entrances of the gates, in the city, she uttereth her words:

²²'How long, ye thoughtless, will ye love thoughtlessness?

And how long will scorners delight them in scorning,

And fools hate knowledge?

²³Turn you at my reproof;

Behold, I will pour out my spirit unto you,

I will make known my words unto you.

²⁴Because I have called, and ye refused,

I have stretched out my hand, and no man attended,

²⁵But ye have set at nought all my counsel,

And would none of my reproof;

²⁶I also, in your calamity, will laugh,

I will mock when your dread cometh;

²⁷When your dread cometh as a storm,

And your calamity cometh on as a whirlwind;

When trouble and distress come upon you.

²⁸Then will they call me, but I will not answer,

They will seek me earnestly, but they shall not find me.

²⁹For that they hated knowledge,

And did not choose the fear of the Lord;

³⁰They would none of my counsel,

They despised all my reproof.

[31]Therefore shall they eat of the fruit of their own way,

And be filled with their own devices.

[32]For the waywardness of the thoughtless shall slay them,

And the confidence of fools shall destroy them.

[33]But whoso hearkeneth unto me shall dwell securely,

And shall be quiet without fear of evil.'

2

My son, if thou wilt receive my words,

And lay up my commandments with thee;

[2]So that thou make thine ear attend unto wisdom,

And thy heart incline to discernment;

[3]Yea, if thou call for understanding,

And lift up thy voice for discernment;

[4]If thou seek her as silver,

And search for her as for hid treasures;

[5]Then shalt thou understand the fear of the Lord,

And find the knowledge of God.

[6]For the Lord giveth wisdom,

Out of His mouth cometh knowledge and discernment;

[7]He layeth up sound wisdom for the upright,

He is a shield to them that walk in integrity;

[8]That He may guard the paths of justice,

And preserve the way of His godly ones.

[9]Then shalt thou understand righteousness and justice,

And equity, yea, every good path.

[10]For wisdom shall enter into thy heart,

And knowledge shall be pleasant unto thy soul;

[11]Discretion shall watch over thee,

Discernment shall guard thee;

[12]To deliver thee from the way of evil,

From the men that speak froward things;

[13]Who leave the paths of uprightness,

To walk in the ways of darkness;

[14]Who rejoice to do evil,

And delight in the frowardness of evil;

[15]Who are crooked in their ways,

And perverse in their paths;

[16]To deliver thee from the strange woman,

Even from the alien woman that maketh smooth her words;

[17]That forsaketh the lord of her youth,

And forgetteth the covenant of her God.

[18]For her house sinketh down unto death,

And her paths unto the shades;

[19]None that go unto her return,

Neither do they attain unto the paths of life;

[20]That thou mayest walk in the way of good men,

And keep the paths of the righteous.

[21]For the upright shall dwell in the land,

And the whole-hearted shall remain in it.

[22]But the wicked shall be cut off from the land,

And the faithless shall be plucked up out of it.

3 My son, forget not my teaching;

But let thy heart keep my commandments;

[2]For length of days, and years of life,

And peace, will they add to thee.

[3]Let not kindness and truth forsake thee;

Bind them about thy neck, write them upon the table of thy heart;

[4]So shalt thou find grace and good favour

In the sight of God and man.

[5]Trust in the Lord with all thy heart,

And lean not upon thine own understanding.

[6]In all thy ways acknowledge Him,

And He will direct thy paths.

[7]Be not wise in thine own eyes;

Fear the Lord, and depart from evil;

[8]It shall be health to thy navel,

And marrow to thy bones.

[9]Honour the Lord with thy substance,

And with the first-fruits of all thine increase; [10]So shall thy barns be filled with plenty,

And thy vats shall overflow with new wine.

[11]My son, despise not the chastening of the Lord,

Neither spurn thou His correction;

[12]For whom the Lord loveth He correcteth,

Even as a father the son in whom he delighteth.

[13]Happy is the man that findeth wisdom,

And the man that obtaineth understanding.

[14]For the merchandise of it is better than the merchandise of silver,

And the gain thereof than fine gold.

[15]She is more precious than rubies;

And all the things thou canst desire are not to be compared unto her.

[16]Length of days is in her right hand;

In her left hand are riches and honour.

[17]Her ways are ways of pleasantness,

And all her paths are peace.

[18]She is a tree of life to them that lay hold upon her,

And happy is every one that holdest her fast.

[19]The Lord by wisdom founded the earth;

By understanding He established the heavens.

[20]By His knowledge the depths were broken up,

And the skies drop down the dew.

²¹My son, let not them depart from thine eyes;

Keep sound wisdom and discretion;

²²So shall they be life unto thy soul,

And grace to thy neck.

²³Then shalt thou walk in thy way securely,

And thou shalt not dash thy foot.

²⁴When thou liest down, thou shalt not be afraid;

Yea, thou shalt lie down, and thy sleep shall be sweet.

²⁵Be not afraid of sudden terror,

Neither of the destruction of the wicked, when it cometh;

²⁶For the Lord will be thy confidence,

And will keep thy foot from being caught.

²⁷Withhold not good from him to whom it is due,

When it is in the power of thy hand to do it.

²⁸Say not unto thy neighbour: 'Go, and come again,

And to-morrow I will give'; when thou hast it by thee.

²⁹Devise not evil against thy neighbour,

Seeing he dwelleth securely by thee.

³⁰Strive not with a man without cause,

If he have done thee no harm.

³¹Envy thou not the man of violence,

And choose none of his ways.

³²For the perverse is an abomination to the Lord;

But His counsel is with the upright.

³³The curse of the Lord is in the house of the wicked;

But He blesseth the habitation of the righteous.

³⁴If it concerneth the scorners, He scorneth them,

But unto the humble He giveth grace.

³⁵The wise shall inherit honour;

But as for the fools, they carry away shame.

4

Hear, ye children, the instruction of a father,

And attend to know understanding.

²For I give you good doctrine;

Forsake ye not my teaching.

³For I was a son unto my father,

Tender and an only one in the sight of my mother.

⁴And he taught me, and said unto me:

'Let thy heart hold fast my words,

Keep my commandments, and live;

⁵Get wisdom, get understanding;

Forget not, neither decline from the words of my mouth;

⁶Forsake her not, and she will preserve thee;

Love her, and she will keep thee.

⁷The beginning of wisdom is: Get wisdom;

Yea, with all thy getting get understanding.

⁸Extol her, and she will exalt thee;

She will bring thee to honour, when thou dost embrace her.

⁹She will give to thy head a chaplet of grace;

A crown of glory will she bestow on thee.'

¹⁰Hear, O my son, and receive my sayings;

And the years of thy life shall be many.

¹¹I have taught thee in the way of wisdom;

I have led thee in paths of uprightness.

¹²When thou goest, thy step shall not be straitened;

And if thou runnest, thou shalt not stumble.

¹³Take fast hold of instruction, let her not go;

Keep her, for she is thy life.

¹⁴Enter not into the path of the wicked,

And walk not in the way of evil men.

¹⁵Avoid it, pass not by it;

Turn from it, and pass on.

¹⁶For they sleep not, except they have done evil;

And their sleep is taken away, unless they cause some to fall.

¹⁷For they eat the bread of wickedness,

And drink the wine of violence. ¹⁸But the path of the righteous is as the light of dawn,

That shineth more and more unto the perfect day.

¹⁹The way of the wicked is as darkness;

They know not at what they stumble.

²⁰My son, attend to my words;

Incline thine ear unto my sayings.

²¹Let them not depart from thine eyes;

Keep them in the midst of thy heart.

²²For they are life unto those that find them,

And health to all their flesh.

²³Above all that thou guardest keep thy heart;

For out of it are the issues of life.

²⁴Put away from thee a froward mouth,

And perverse lips put far from thee.

²⁵Let thine eyes look right on,

And let thine eyelids look straight before thee.

²⁶Make plain the path of thy feet,

And let all thy ways be established.

²⁷Turn not to the right hand nor to the left;

Remove thy foot from evil.

5 My son, attend unto my wisdom;

Incline thine ear to my understanding;

²That thou mayest preserve discretion,

And that thy lips may keep knowledge.

³For the lips of a strange woman drop honey,

And her mouth is smoother than oil;

[4]But her end is bitter as wormwood,

Sharp as a two-edged sword.

[5]Her feet go down to death;

Her steps take hold on the nether-world;

[6]Lest she should walk the even path of life,

Her ways wander, but she knoweth it not.

[7]Now therefore, O ye children, hearken unto me,

And depart not from the words of my mouth.

[8]Remove thy way far from her,

And come not nigh the door of her house;

[9]Lest thou give thy vigour unto others,

And thy years unto the cruel;

[10]Lest strangers be filled with thy strength,

And thy labours be in the house of an alien;

[11]And thou moan, when thine end cometh,

When thy flesh and thy body are consumed,

[12]And say: 'How have I hated instruction,

And my heart despised reproof;

[13]Neither have I hearkened to the voice of my teachers,

Nor inclined mine ear to them that instructed me!

[14]I was well nigh in all evil In the midst of the congregation and assembly.'

[15]Drink waters out of thine own cistern,

And running waters out of thine own well.

[16]Let thy springs be dispersed abroad,

And courses of water in the streets.

[17]Let them be only thine own,

And not strangers' with thee.

[18]Let thy fountain be blessed;

And have joy of the wife of thy youth.

[19]A lovely hind and a graceful doe,

Let her breasts satisfy thee at all times;

With her love be thou ravished always.

[20]Why then wilt thou, my son, be ravished with a strange woman,

And embrace the bosom of an alien?

[21]For the ways of man are before the eyes of the Lord,

And He maketh even all his paths.

[22]His own iniquities shall ensnare the wicked,

And he shall be holden with the cords of his sin.

[23]He shall die for lack of instruction;

And in the greatness of his folly he shall reel.

6 My son, if thou art become surety for thy neighbour,

If thou hast struck thy hands for a stranger—

[2]Thou art snared by the words of thy mouth,

Thou art caught by the words of thy mouth—

[3]Do this now, my son, and deliver thyself,

Seeing thou art come into the hand of thy neighbour;

Go, humble thyself, and urge thy neighbour.

[4]Give not sleep to thine eyes,

nor slumber to thine eyelids.

[5]Deliver thyself as a gazelle from the hand [of the hunter],

And as a bird from the hand of the fowler.

[6]Go to the ant, thou sluggard;

Consider her ways, and be wise;

[7]Which having no chief,

Overseer, or ruler,

[8]Provideth her bread in the summer,

And gatherest her food in the harvest.

[9]How long wilt thou sleep, O sluggard?

When wilt thou arise out of thy sleep?

[10]'Yet a little sleep, a little slumber,

A little folding of the hands to sleep'—

[11]So shall thy poverty come as a runner,

And thy want as an armed man.

[12]A base person, a man of iniquity,

Is he that walketh with a froward mouth;

[13]That winketh with his eyes, that scrapeth with his feet,

That pointeth with his fingers;

[14]Frowardness is in his heart, he deviseth evil continually;

He soweth discord.

[15]Therefore shall his calamity come suddenly;

On a sudden shall he be broken, and that without remedy.

[16]There are six things which the Lord hateth,

Yea, seven which are an abomination unto Him:

[17]Haughty eyes, a lying tongue,

And hands that shed innocent blood;

[18]A heart that deviseth wicked thoughts,

Feet that are swift in running to evil;

[19]A false witness that breatheth out lies,

And he that soweth discord among brethren.

[20]My son, keep the commandment of thy father,

And forsake not the teaching of thy mother;

[21]Bind them continually upon thy heart,

Tie them about thy neck.

[22]When thou walkest, it shall lead thee,

When thou liest down, it shall watch over thee;

And when thou awakest, it shall talk with thee.

[23]For the commandment is a lamp, and the teaching is light,

And reproofs of instruction are the way of life;

[24]To keep thee from the evil woman,

From the smoothness of the alien tongue.

²⁵Lust not after her beauty in thy heart;

Neither let her captivate thee with her eyelids.

²⁶For on account of a harlot a man is brought to a loaf of bread,

But the adulteress hunteth for the precious life.

²⁷Can a man take fire in his bosom,

And his clothes not be burned?

²⁸Or can one walk upon hot coals,

And his feet not be scorched?

²⁹So he that goeth in to his neighbour's wife;

Whosoever toucheth her shall not go unpunished.

³⁰Men do not despise a thief, if he steal

To satisfy his soul when he is hungry;

³¹But if he be found, he must restore sevenfold,

He must give all the substance of his house.

³²He that committeth adultery with a woman lacketh understanding;

He doeth it that would destroy his own soul.

³³Wounds and dishonour shall he get,

And his reproach shall not be wiped away.

³⁴For jealousy is the rage of a man,

And he will not spare in the day of vengeance.

³⁵He will not regard any ransom;

Neither will he rest content, though thou givest many gifts.

7 My son, keep my words,

And lay up my commandments with thee.

²Keep my commandments and live,

And my teaching as the apple of thine eye.

³Bind them upon thy fingers,

Write them upon the table of thy heart.

⁴Say unto wisdom: 'Thou art my sister',

And call understanding thy kinswoman;

[5]That they may keep thee from the strange woman,

From the alien woman that maketh smooth her words.

[6]For at the window of my house

I looked forth through my lattice;

[7]And I beheld among the thoughtless ones,

I discerned among the youths,

A young man void of understanding,

[8]Passing through the street near her corner,

And he went the way to her house;

[9]In the twilight, in the evening of the day,

In the blackness of night and the darkness.

[10]And, behold, there met him a woman

With the attire of a harlot, and wily of heart.

[11]She is riotous and rebellious,

Her feet abide not in her house;

[12]Now she is in the streets, now in the broad places,

And lieth in wait at every corner.

[13]So she caught him, and kissed him,

And with an impudent face she said unto him:

[14]'Sacrifices of peace-offerings were due from me;

This day have I paid my vows.

[15]Therefore came I forth to meet thee,

To seek thy face, and I have found thee.

[16]I have decked my couch with coverlets,

With striped cloths of the yarn of Egypt.

[17]I have perfumed my bed

With myrrh, aloes, and cinnamon.

[18]Come, let us take our fill of love until the morning;

Let us solace ourselves with loves.

[19]For my husband is not at home,

He is gone a long journey;

[20]He hath taken the bag of money with him;

He will come home at the full moon.'

[21]With her much fair speech she causeth him to yield,

With the blandishment of her lips she enticeth him away.

[22]He goeth after her straightway,

As an ox that goeth to the slaughter,

Or as one in fetters to the correction of the fool;

[23]Till an arrow strike through his liver;

As a bird hasteneth to the snare—

And knoweth not that it is at the cost of his life.

[24]Now therefore, O ye children, hearken unto me,

And attend to the words of my mouth.

[25]Let not thy heart decline to her ways,

Go not astray in her paths.

[26]For she hath cast down many wounded;

Yea, a mighty host are all her slain.

[27]Her house is the way to the nether-world,

Going down to the chambers of death.

8 Doth not wisdom call,

And understanding put forth her voice?

[2]In the top of high places by the way,

Where the paths meet, she standeth;

[3]Beside the gates, at the entry of the city,

At the coming in at the doors, she crieth aloud:

[4]'Unto you, O men, I call,

And my voice is to the sons of men.

[5]O ye thoughtless, understand prudence,

And, ye fools, be ye of an understanding heart.

⁶Hear, for I will speak excellent things,

And the opening of my lips shall be right things.

⁷For my mouth shall utter truth,

And wickedness is an abomination to my lips.

⁸All the words of my mouth are in righteousness,

There is nothing perverse or crooked in them.

⁹They are all plain to him that understandeth,

And right to them that find knowledge.

¹⁰Receive my instruction, and not silver,

And knowledge rather than choice gold.

¹¹For wisdom is better than rubies,

And all things desirable are not to be compared unto her.

¹²I wisdom dwell with prudence,

And find out knowledge of devices.

¹³The fear of the Lord is to hate evil;

Pride, and arrogancy, and the evil way,

And the froward mouth, do I hate.

¹⁴Counsel is mine, and sound wisdom;

I am understanding, power is mine.

¹⁵By me kings reign,

And princes decree justice.

¹⁶By me princes rule, And nobles, even all the judges of the earth.

¹⁷I love them that love me,

And those that seek me earnestly shall find me.

¹⁸Riches and honour are with me;

Yea, enduring riches and righteousness.

¹⁹My fruit is better than gold, yea, than fine gold;

And my produce than choice silver.

²⁰I walk in the way of righteousness,

In the midst of the paths of justice;

²¹That I may cause those that love me to inherit substance,

And that I may fill their treasuries.

²²The Lord made me as the beginning of His way,

The first of His works of old.

²³I was set up from everlasting, from the beginning,

Or ever the earth was.

²⁴When there were no depths, I was brought forth;

When there were no fountains abounding with water.

²⁵Before the mountains were settled,

Before the hills was I brought forth;

²⁶While as yet He had not made the earth, nor the fields,

Nor the beginning of the dust of the world.

²⁷When He established the heavens, I was there;

When He set a circle upon the face of the deep,

²⁸When He made firm the skies above,

When the fountains of the deep showed their might,

²⁹When He gave to the sea His decree,

That the waters should not transgress His commandment,

When He appointed the foundations of the earth;

³⁰Then I was by Him, as a nursling;

And I was daily all delight,

Playing always before Him,

³¹Playing in His habitable earth,

And my delights are with the sons of men.

³²Now therefore, ye children, hearken unto me;

For happy are they that keep my ways.

³³Hear instruction, and be wise,

And refuse it not.

³⁴Happy is the man that hearkeneth to me,

Watching daily at my gates, waiting at the posts of my doors.

³⁵For whoso findeth me findeth life,

And obtaineth favour of the Lord.

³⁶But he that misseth me wrongeth his own soul;

All they that hate me love death.'

9 Wisdom hath builded her house,

She hath hewn out her seven pillars;

²She hath prepared her meat, she hath mingled her wine;

She hath also furnished her table.

³She hath sent forth her maidens, she calleth,

Upon the highest places of the city:

⁴'Whoso is thoughtless, let him turn in hither';

As for him that lacketh understanding, she saith to him:

⁵'Come, eat of my bread,

And drink of the wine which I have mingled.

⁶Forsake all thoughtlessness, and live;

And walk in the way of understanding.

⁷He that correcteth a scorner getteth to himself shame,

And he that reproveth a wicked man, it becometh unto him a blot.

⁸Reprove not a scorner, lest he hate thee;

Reprove a wise man, and he will love thee.

⁹Give to a wise man, and he will be yet wiser;

Teach a righteous man, and he will increase in learning.

¹⁰The fear of the Lord is the beginning of wisdom,

And the knowledge of the All-holy is understanding.

¹¹For by me thy days shall be multiplied,

And the years of thy life shall be increased.

¹²If thou art wise, thou art wise for thyself;

And if thou scornest, thou alone shalt bear it.'

¹³The woman Folly is riotous;

She is thoughtless, and knoweth nothing.

¹⁴And she sitteth at the door of her house,

On a seat in the high places of the city,

15To call to them that pass by,

Who go right on their ways:

16'Whoso is thoughtless, let him turn in hither';

And as for him that lacketh understanding, she saith to him:

17'Stolen waters are sweet,

And bread eaten in secret is pleasant.'

18But he knoweth not that the shades are there;

That her guests are in the depths of the nether-world.

10 The proverbs of Solomon.

A wise son maketh a glad father;

But a foolish son is the grief of his mother.

2Treasures of wickedness profit nothing;

But righteousness delivereth from death.

3The Lord will not suffer the soul of the righteous to famish;

But He thrusteth away the desire of the wicked.

4He becometh poor that dealeth with a slack hand; But the hand of the diligent maketh rich.

5A wise son gathereth in summer;

But a son that doeth shamefully sleepeth in harvest.

6Blessings are upon the head of the righteous;

But the mouth of the wicked concealeth violence.

7The memory of the righteous shall be for a blessing;

But the name of the wicked shall rot.

8The wise in heart will receive commandments;

But a prating fool shall fall.

9He that walketh uprightly walketh securely;

But he that perverteth his ways shall be found out.

10He that winketh with the eye causeth sorrow;

And a prating fool shall fall.

¹¹The mouth of the righteous is a fountain of life;

But the mouth of the wicked concealeth violence.

¹²Hatred stirreth up strifes;

But love covereth all transgressions.

¹³In the lips of him that hath discernment wisdom is found;

But a rod is for the back of him that is void of understanding.

¹⁴Wise men lay up knowledge;

But the mouth of the foolish is an imminent ruin.

¹⁵The rich man's wealth is his strong city;

The ruin of the poor is their poverty.

¹⁶The wages of the righteous is life;

The increase of the wicked is sin.

¹⁷He is in the way of life that heedeth instruction;

But he that forsaketh reproof erreth.

¹⁸He that hideth hatred is of lying lips;

And he that uttereth a slander is a fool.

¹⁹In the multitude of words there wanteth not transgression;

But he that refraineth his lips is wise.

²⁰The tongue of the righteous is as choice silver;

The heart of the wicked is little worth.

²¹The lips of the righteous feed many;

But the foolish die for want of understanding.

²²The blessing of the Lord, it maketh rich,

And toil addeth nothing thereto.

²³It is as sport to a fool to do wickedness,

And so is wisdom to a man of discernment.

²⁴The fear of the wicked, it shall come upon him;

And the desire of the righteous shall be granted.

²⁵When the whirlwind passeth, the wicked is no more;

But the righteous is an everlasting foundation.

²⁶As vinegar to the teeth, and as smoke to the eyes,

So is the sluggard to them that send him.

27The fear of the Lord prolongeth days;

But the years of the wicked shall be shortened.

28The hope of the righteous is gladness;

But the expectation of the wicked shall perish.

29The way of the Lord is a stronghold to the upright,

But ruin to the workers of iniquity.

30The righteous shall never be moved;

But the wicked shall not inhabit the land.

31The mouth of the righteous buddeth with wisdom;

But the froward tongue shall be cut off.

32The lips of the righteous know what is acceptable;

But the mouth of the wicked is all frowardness.

11 A false balance is an abomination to the Lord,

But a perfect weight is His delight.

2When pride cometh, then cometh shame;

But with the lowly is wisdom.

3The integrity of the upright shall guide them;

But the perverseness of the faithless shall destroy them.

4Riches profit not in the day of wrath;

But righteousness delivereth from death.

5The righteousness of the sincere shall make straight his way;

But the wicked shall fall by his own wickedness.

6The righteousness of the upright shall deliver them;

But the faithless shall be trapped in their own crafty device.

7When a wicked man dieth, his expectation shall perish,

And the hope of strength perisheth.

8The righteous is delivered out of trouble,

And the wicked cometh in his stead.

[9]With his mouth the impious man destroyeth his neighbour;

But through knowledge shall the righteous be delivered.

[10]When it goeth well with the righteous, the city rejoiceth;

And when the wicked perish, there is joy.

[11]By the blessing of the upright a city is exalted;

But it is overthrown by the mouth of the wicked.

[12]He that despiseth his neighbour lacketh understanding;

But a man of discernment holdeth his peace.

[13]He that goeth about as a talebearer revealeth secrets;

But he that is of a faithful spirit concealeth a matter.

[14]Where no wise direction is, a people falleth;

But in the multitude of counsellors there is safety.

[15]He that is surety for a stranger shall smart for it;

But he that hateth them that strike hands is secure.

[16]A gracious woman obtaineth honour;

And strong men obtain riches.

[17]The merciful man doeth good to his own soul;

But he that is cruel troubleth his own flesh.

[18]The wicked earneth deceitful wages;

But he that soweth righteousness hath a sure reward.

[19]Stedfast righteousness tendeth to life;

But he that pursueth evil pursueth it to his own death.

[20]They that are perverse in heart are an abomination to the Lord;

But such as are upright in their way are His delight.

[21]My hand upon it! the evil man shall not be unpunished;

But the seed of the righteous shall escape.

[22]As a ring of gold in a swine's snout, so is a fair woman that turneth aside from discretion.

[23]The desire of the righteous is only good;

But the expectation of the wicked is wrath.

[24]There is that scattereth, and yet increaseth;

And there is that withholdeth more than is meet, but it tendeth only to want.

²⁵The beneficent soul shall be made rich,

And he that satisfieth abundantly shall be satisfied also himself.

²⁶He that withholdeth corn, the people shall curse him;

But blessing shall be upon the head of him that selleth it.

²⁷He that diligently seeketh good seeketh favour;

But he that searcheth for evil, it shall come unto him.

²⁸He that trusteth in his riches shall fall;

But the righteous shall flourish as foliage.

²⁹He that troubleth his own house shall inherit the wind;

And the foolish shall be servant to the wise of heart.

³⁰The fruit of the righteous is a tree of life;

And he that is wise winneth souls.

³¹Behold, the righteous shall be requited in the earth;

How much more the wicked and the sinner!

12 Whoso loveth knowledge loveth correction;

But he that is brutish hateth reproof.

²A good man shall obtain favour of the Lord;

But a man of wicked devices will He condemn.

³A man shall not be established by wickedness;

But the root of the righteous shall never be moved.

⁴A virtuous woman is a crown to her husband;

But she that doeth shamefully is as rottenness in his bones.

⁵The thoughts of the righteous are right;

But the counsels of the wicked are deceit.

⁶The words of the wicked are to lie in wait for blood;

But the mouth of the upright shall deliver them.

⁷The wicked are overthrown, and are not;

But the house of the righteous shall stand.

⁸A man shall be commended according to his intelligence;

But he that is of a distorted understanding shall be despised.

⁹Better is he that is lightly esteemed, and hath a servant,

Than he that playeth the man of rank, and lacketh bread.

¹⁰A righteous man regardeth the life of his beast;

But the tender mercies of the wicked are cruel.

¹¹He that tilleth his ground shall have plenty of bread;

But he that followeth after vain things is void of understanding.

¹²The wicked desireth the prey of evil men;

But the root of the righteous yieldeth fruit.

¹³In the transgression of the lips is a snare to the evil man;

But the righteous cometh out of trouble.

¹⁴A man shall be satisfied with good by the fruit of his mouth,

And the doings of a man's hands shall be rendered unto him.

¹⁵The way of a fool is straight in his own eyes;

But he that is wise hearkeneth unto counsel.

¹⁶A fool's vexation is presently known;

But a prudent man concealeth shame.

¹⁷He that breatheth forth truth uttereth righteousness;

But a false witness deceit.

¹⁸There is that speaketh like the piercings of a sword;

But the tongue of the wise is health.

¹⁹The lip of truth shall be established for ever;

But a lying tongue is but for a moment.

²⁰Deceit is in the heart of them that devise evil;

But to the counsellors of peace is joy.

²¹There shall no mischief befall the righteous;

But the wicked are filled with evil.

²²Lying lips are an abomination to the Lord;

But they that deal truly are His delight.

²³A prudent man concealeth knowledge;

But the heart of fools proclaimeth foolishness.

24The hand of the diligent shall bear rule;

But the slothful shall be under tribute.

25Care in the heart of a man boweth it down;

But a good word maketh it glad.

26The righteous is guided by his friend;

But the way of the wicked leadeth them astray.

27The slothful man shall not hunt his prey;

But the precious substance of men is to be diligent.

28In the way of righteousness is life,

And in the pathway thereof there is no death.

13 A wise son is instructed of his father;

But a scorner heareth not rebuke.

2A man shall eat good from the fruit of his mouth;

But the desire of the faithless is violence.

3He that guardeth his mouth keepeth his life;

But for him that openeth wide his lips there shall be ruin.

4The soul of the sluggard desireth, and hath nothing;

But the soul of the diligent shall be abundantly gratified.

5A righteous man hateth lying;

But a wicked man behaveth vilely and shamefully.

6Righteousness guardeth him that is upright in the way;

But wickedness overthroweth the sinner.

7There is that pretendeth himself rich, yet hath nothing;

There is that pretendeth himself poor, yet hath great wealth.

8The ransom of a man's life are his riches;

But the poor heareth no threatening.

9The light of the righteous rejoiceth;

But the lamp of the wicked shall be put out.

10By pride cometh only contention;

But with the well-advised is wisdom.

[11]Wealth gotten by vanity shall be diminished;

But he that gathereth little by little shall increase.

[12]Hope deferred maketh the heart sick;

But desire fulfilled is a tree of life.

[13]Whoso despiseth the word shall suffer thereby;

But he that feareth the commandment shall be rewarded.

[14]The teaching of the wise is a fountain of life,

To depart from the snares of death.

[15]Good understanding giveth grace;

But the way of the faithless is harsh.

[16]Every prudent man dealeth with forethought;

But a fool unfoldeth folly.

[17]A wicked messenger falleth into evil;

But a faithful ambassador is health.

[18]Poverty and shame shall be to him that refuseth instruction;

But he that regardeth reproof shall be honoured.

[19]The desire accomplished is sweet to the soul;

And it is an abomination to fools to depart from evil.

[20]He that walketh with wise men shall be wise;

But the companion of fools shall smart for it.

[21]Evil pursueth sinners;

But to the righteous good shall be repaid.

[22]A good man leaveth an inheritance to his children's children;

And the wealth of the sinner is laid up for the righteous.

[23]Much food is in the tillage of the poor;

But there is that is swept away by want of righteousness.

[24]He that spareth his rod hateth his son;

But he that loveth him chasteneth him betimes.

[25]The righteous eateth to the satisfying of his desire;

But the belly of the wicked shall want.

14

Every wise woman buildeth her house;

But the foolish plucketh it down with her hands.

²He that walketh in his uprightness feareth the Lord;

But he that is perverse in his ways despiseth Him.

³In the mouth of the foolish is a rod of pride;

But the lips of the wise shall preserve them.

⁴Where no oxen are, the crib is clean;

But much increase is by the strength of the ox.

⁵A faithful witness will not lie;

But a false witness breatheth forth lies.

⁶A scorner seeketh wisdom, and findeth it not;

But knowledge is easy unto him that hath discernment.

⁷Go from the presence of a foolish man, for thou wilt not perceive the lips of knowledge.

⁸The wisdom of the prudent is to look well to his way;

But the folly of fools is deceit.

⁹Amends pleadeth for fools;

But among the upright there is good will.

¹⁰The heart knoweth its own bitterness;

And with its joy no stranger can intermeddle.

¹¹The house of the wicked shall be overthrown;

But the tent of the upright shall flourish.

¹²There is a way which seemeth right unto a man,

But the end thereof are the ways of death.

¹³Even in laughter the heart acheth;

And the end of mirth is heaviness.

¹⁴The dissembler in heart shall have his fill from his own ways;

And a good man shall be satisfied from himself.

¹⁵The thoughtless believeth every word;

But the prudent man looketh well to his going.

[16]A wise man feareth, and departeth from evil;

But the fool behaveth overbearingly, and is confident.

[17]He that is soon angry dealeth foolishly;

And a man of wicked devices is hated.

[18]The thoughtless come into possession of folly;

But the prudent are crowned with knowledge.

[19]The evil bow before the good,

And the wicked at the gates of the righteous.

[20]The poor is hated even of his own neighbour;

But the rich hath many friends.

[21]He that despiseth his neighbour sinneth;

But he that is gracious unto the humble, happy is he.

[22]Shall they not go astray that devise evil? But mercy and truth shall be for them that devise good.

[23]In all labour there is profit;

But the talk of the lips tendeth only to penury.

[24]The crown of the wise is their riches;

But the folly of fools remaineth folly.

[25]A true witness delivereth souls;

But he that breatheth forth lies is all deceit.

[26]In the fear of the Lord a man hath strong confidence;

And his children shall have a place of refuge.

[27]The fear of the Lord is a fountain of life, to depart from the snares of death.

[28]In the multitude of people is the king's glory;

But in the want of people is the ruin of the prince.

[29]He that is slow to anger is of great understanding;

But he that is hasty of spirit exalteth folly.

[30]A tranquil heart is the life of the flesh;

But envy is the rottenness of the bones.

[31]He that oppresseth the poor blasphemeth his Maker;

But he that is gracious unto the needy honoureth Him.

[32]The wicked is thrust down in his misfortune;

But the righteous, even when he is brought to death, hath hope.

[33]In the heart of him that hath discernment wisdom resteth;

But in the inward part of fools it maketh itself known.

[34]Righteousness exalteth a nation;

But sin is a reproach to any people.

[35]The king's favour is toward a servant that dealeth wisely;

But his wrath striketh him that dealeth shamefully.

15 A soft answer turneth away wrath;

But a grievous word stirreth up anger.

[2]The tongue of the wise useth knowledge aright; But the mouth of fools poureth out foolishness.

[3]The eyes of the Lord are in every place,

Keeping watch upon the evil and the good.

[4]A soothing tongue is a tree of life;

But perverseness therein is a wound to the spirit.

[5]A fool despiseth his father's correction;

But he that regardeth reproof is prudent.

[6]In the house of the righteous is much treasure;

But in the revenues of the wicked is trouble.

[7]The lips of the wise disperse knowledge;

But the heart of the foolish is not stedfast.

[8]The sacrifice of the wicked is an abomination to the Lord;

But the prayer of the upright is His delight.

[9]The way of the wicked is an abomination to the Lord;

But He loveth him that followeth after righteousness.

[10]There is grievous correction for him that forsaketh the way;

And he that hateth reproof shall die.

[11]The nether-world and Destruction are before the Lord;

How much more then the hearts of the children of men!

[12]A scorner loveth not to be reproved;

He will not go unto the wise.

[13]A merry heart maketh a cheerful countenance;

But by sorrow of heart the spirit is broken.

[14]The heart of him that hath discernment seeketh knowledge;

But the mouth of fools feedeth on folly.

[15]All the days of the poor are evil;

But he that is of a merry heart hath a continual feast.

[16]Better is little with the fear of the Lord,

Than great treasure and turmoil therewith.

[17]Better is a dinner of herbs where love is,

Than a stalled ox and hatred therewith.

[18]A wrathful man stirreth up discord;

But he that is slow to anger appeaseth strife.

[19]The way of the sluggard is as though hedged by thorns;

But the path of the upright is even.

[20]A wise son maketh a glad father;

But a foolish man despiseth his mother.

[21]Folly is joy to him that lacketh understanding;

But a man of discernment walketh straightforwards.

[22]For want of counsel purposes are frustrated;

But in the multitude of counsellors they are established.

[23]A man hath joy in the answer of his mouth;

And a word in due season, how good is it!

[24]The path of life goeth upward for the wise, that he may depart from the nether-world beneath.

[25]The Lord will pluck up the house of the proud;

But He will establish the border of the widow.

[26]The thoughts of wickedness are an abomination to the Lord;

But words of pleasantness are pure.

[27]He that is greedy of gain troubleth his own house;

But he that hateth gifts shall live.

28The heart of the righteous studieth to answer;

But the mouth of the wicked poureth out evil things.

29The Lord is far from the wicked;

But He heareth the prayer of the righteous.

30The light of the eyes rejoiceth the heart;

And a good report maketh the bones fat.

31The ear that hearkeneth to the reproof of life abideth among the wise.

32He that refuseth correction despiseth his own soul;

But he that hearkeneth to reproof getteth understanding.

33The fear of the Lord is the instruction of wisdom;

And before honour goeth humility.

16 The preparations of the heart are man's,

But the answer of the tongue is from the Lord.

2All the ways of a man are clean in his own eyes;

But the Lord weigheth the spirits.

3Commit thy works unto the Lord, And thy thoughts shall be established.

4The Lord hath made every things for His own purpose,

Yea, even the wicked for the day of evil.

5Every one that is proud in heart is an abomination to the Lord;

My hand upon it! he shall not be unpunished.

6By mercy and truth iniquity is expiated;

And by the fear of the Lord men depart from evil.

7When a man's ways please the Lord,

He maketh even his enemies to be at peace with him.

8Better is a little with righteousness

Than great revenues with injustice.

9A man's heart deviseth his way;

But the Lord directeth his steps.

10A divine sentence is in the lips of the king;

His mouth trespasseth not in judgment.

[11]A just balance and scales are the Lord's;

All the weights of the bag are His work.

[12]It is an abomination to kings to commit wickedness;

For the throne is established by righteousness.

[13]Righteous lips are the delight of kings;

And they love him that speaketh right.

[14]The wrath of a king is as messengers of death;

But a wise man will pacify it.

[15]In the light of the king's countenance is life;

And his favour is as a cloud of the latter rain.

[16]How much better is it to get wisdom than gold!

Yea, to get understanding is rather to be chosen than silver.

[17]The highway of the upright is to depart from evil;

He that keepeth his way preserveth his soul.

[18]Pride goeth before destruction,

And a haughty spirit before a fall.

[19]Better it is to be of a lowly spirit with the humble,

Than to divide the spoil with the proud.

[20]He that giveth heed unto the word shall find good;

And whoso trusteth in the Lord, happy is he.

[21]The wise in heart is called a man of discernment;

And the sweetness of the lips increaseth learning.

[22]Understanding is a fountain of life unto him that hath it;

But folly is the chastisement of fools.

[23]The heart of the wise teacheth his mouth,

And addeth learning to his lips.

[24]Pleasant words are as a honeycomb,

Sweet to the soul, and health to the bones.

[25]There is a way which seemeth right unto a man,

But the end thereof are the ways of death.

²⁶The hunger of the labouring man laboureth for him;

For his mouth compelleth him.

²⁷An ungodly man diggeth up evil,

And in his lips there is as a burning fire.

²⁸A froward man soweth strife;

And a whisperer separateth familiar friends.

²⁹A man of violence enticeth his neighbour,

And leadeth him into a way that is not good.

³⁰He shutteth his eyes, it is to devise froward things;

He that biteth his lips bringeth evil to pass.

³¹The hoary head is a crown of glory,

It is found in the way of righteousness.

³²He that is slow to anger is better than the mighty;

And he that ruleth his spirit than he that taketh a city.

³³The lot is cast into the lap;

But the whole disposing thereof is of the Lord.

17 Better is a dry morsel and quietness therewith,

Than a house full of feasting with strife.

²A servant that dealeth wisely shall have rule over a son that dealeth shamefully,

And shall have part of the inheritance among the brethren.

³The refining pot is for silver, and the furnace for gold;

But the Lord trieth the hearts.

⁴A evil-doer giveth heed to wicked lips;

And a liar giveth ear to a mischievous tongue.

⁵Whoso mocketh the poor blasphemeth his Maker;

And he that is glad at calamity shall not be unpunished.

⁶Children's children are the crown of old men;

And the glory of children are their fathers.

⁷Overbearing speech becometh not a churl;

Much less do lying lips a prince.

8A gift is as a precious stone in the eyes of him that hath it;

Whithersoever he turneth, he prospereth.

9He that covereth a transgression seeketh love;

But he that harpeth on a matter estrangeth a familiar friend.

10A rebuke entereth deeper into a man of understanding

Than a hundred stripes into a fool.

11A rebellious man seeketh only evil;

Therefore a cruel messenger shall be sent against him.

12Let a bear robbed of her whelps meet a man,

Rather than a fool in his folly.

13Whoso rewardeth evil for good,

Evil shall not depart from his house.

14The beginning of strife is as when one letteth out water;

Therefore leave off contention, before the quarrel break out.

15He that justifieth the wicked, and he that condemneth the righteous,

Even they both are an abomination to the Lord.

16Wherefore is there a price in the hand of a fool

To buy wisdom, seeing he hath no understanding?

17A friend loveth at all times,

And a brother is born for adversity.

18A man void of understanding is he that striketh hands,

And becometh surety in the presence of his neighbour.

19He loveth transgression that loveth strife;

He that exalteth his gate seeketh destruction.

20He that hath a froward heart findeth no good;

And he that hath a perverse tongue falleth into evil.

21He that begetteth a fool doeth it to his sorrow;

And the father of a churl hath no joy.

22A merry heart is a good medicine;

But a broken spirit drieth the bones.

²³A wicked man taketh a gift out of the bosom,

To pervert the ways of justice.

²⁴Wisdom is before him that hath understanding;

But the eyes of a fool are in the ends of the earth.

²⁵A foolish son is vexation to his father,

And bitterness to her that bore him.

²⁶To punish also the righteous is not good,

Nor to strike the noble for their uprightness.

²⁷He that spareth his words hath knowledge;

And he that husbandeth his spirit is a man of discernment.

²⁸Even a fool, when he holdeth his peace, is counted wise;

And he that shutteth his lips is esteemed as a man of understanding.

18 He that separateth himself seeketh his own desire,

And snarlest against all sound wisdom.

²A fool hath no delight in understanding,

But only that his heart may lay itself bare.

³When the wicked cometh, there cometh also contempt,

And with ignominy reproach.

⁴The words of a man's mouth are as deep waters;

A flowing brook, a fountain of wisdom.

⁵It is not good to respect the person of the wicked,

So as to turn aside the righteous in judgment.

⁶A fool's lips enter into contention,

And his mouth calleth for strokes.

⁷A fool's mouth is his ruin,

And his lips are the snare of his soul.

⁸The words of a whisperer are as dainty morsels,

And they go down into the innermost parts of the belly.

⁹Even one that is slack in his work

Is brother to him that is a destroyer.

¹⁰The name of the Lord is a strong tower:

The righteous runneth into it, and is set up on high.

¹¹The rich man's wealth is his strong city,

And as a high wall in his own conceit.

¹²Before destruction the heart of a man is haughty,

And before honour goeth humility.

¹³He that giveth answer before he heareth,

It is folly and confusion unto him.

¹⁴The spirit of a man will sustain his infirmity;

But a broken spirit who can bear?

¹⁵The heart of the prudent getteth knowledge;

And the ear of the wise seeketh knowledge.

¹⁶A man's gift maketh room for him,

And bringeth him before great men.

¹⁷He that pleadeth his cause first seemeth just;

But his neighbour cometh and searcheth him out.

¹⁸The lot causeth strife to cease,

And parteth asunder the contentious.

¹⁹A brother offended is harder to be won than a strong city;

And their contentions are like the bars of a castle.

²⁰A man's belly shall be filled with the fruit of his mouth;

With the increase of his lips shall he be satisfied.

²¹Death and life are in the power of the tongue;

And they that indulge it shall eat the fruit thereof.

²²Whoso findeth a wife findeth a great good,

And obtaineth favour of the Lord.

²³The poor useth entreaties;

But the rich answereth impudently.

²⁴There are friends that one hath to his own hurt;

But there is a friend that sticketh closer than a brother.

19 Better is the poor that walketh in his integrity

Than he that is perverse in his lips and a fool at the same time.

²Also, that the soul be without knowledge is not good;

And he that hasteth with his feet sinneth.

³The foolishness of man perverteth his way;

And his heart fretteth against the Lord.

⁴Wealth addeth many friends;

But as for the poor, his friend separateth himself from him.

⁵A false witness shall not be unpunished;

And he that breatheth forth lies shall not escape.

⁶Many will entreat the favour of the liberal man;

And every man is a friend to him that giveth gifts.

⁷All the brethren of the poor do hate him;

How much more do his friends go far from him!

He that pursueth words, they turn against him.

⁸He that getteth wisdom loveth his own soul;

He that keepeth understanding shall find good.

⁹A false witness shall not be unpunished;

And he that breatheth forth lies shall perish.

¹⁰Luxury is not seemly for a fool;

Much less for a servant to have rule over princes.

¹¹It is the discretion of a man to be slow to anger,

And it is his glory to pass over a transgression.

¹²The king's wrath is as the roaring of a lion;

But his favour is as dew upon the grass.

¹³A foolish son is the calamity of his father;

And the contentions of a wife are a continual dropping.

¹⁴House and riches are the inheritance of fathers;

But a prudent wife is from the Lord.

¹⁵Slothfulness casteth into a deep sleep;

And the idle soul shall suffer hunger.

¹⁶He that keepeth the commandment keepeth his soul;

But he that despiseth His ways shall die.

¹⁷He that is gracious unto the poor lendeth unto the Lord;

And his good deed will He repay unto him.

¹⁸Chasten thy son, for there is hope;

But set not thy heart on his destruction.

¹⁹A man of great wrath shall suffer punishment;

For if thou interpose, thou wilt add thereto.

²⁰Hear counsel, and receive instruction,

That thou mayest be wise in thy latter end.

²¹There are many devices in a man's heart;

But the counsel of the Lord, that shall stand.

²²The lust of a man is his shame;

And a poor man is better than a liar.

²³The fear of the Lord tendeth to life;

And he that hath it shall abide satisfied,

He shall not be visited with evil.

²⁴The sluggard burieth his hand in the dish,

And will not so much as bring it back to his mouth.

²⁵When thou smitest a scorner, the simple will become prudent;

And when one that hath understanding is reproved, he will understand knowledge.

²⁶A son that dealeth shamefully and reproachfully

Will despoil his father, and chase away his mother.

²⁷Cease, my son, to hear the instruction

That causeth to err from the words of knowledge.

²⁸An ungodly witness mocketh at right;

And the mouth of the wicked devoureth iniquity.

²⁹Judgments are prepared for scorners,

And stripes for the back of fools.

20 Wine is a mocker, strong drink is riotous;

And whosoever reeleth thereby is not wise.

2The terror of a king is as the roaring of a lion:

He that provoketh him to anger forfeiteth his life.

3It is an honour for a man to keep aloof from strife;

But every fool will be snarling.

4The sluggard will not plow when winter setteth in;

Therefore he shall beg in harvest, and have nothing.

5Counsel in the heart of man is like deep water;

But a man of understanding will draw it out.

6Most men will proclaim every one his own goodness;

But a faithful man who can find?

7He that walketh in his integrity as a just man,

Happy are his children after him.

8A king that sitteth on the throne of judgment

Scattereth away all evil with his eyes.

9Who can say: 'I have made my heart clean,

I am pure from my sin'?

10Divers weights, and divers measures,

Both of them alike are abomination to the Lord.

11Even a child is known by his doings,

Whether his work be pure, and whether it be right.

12The hearing ear, and the seeing eye,

The Lord hath made even both of them.

13Love not sleep, lest thou come to poverty;

Open thine eyes, and thou shalt have bread in plenty.

14'It is bad, it is bad', saith the buyer;

But when he is gone his way, then he boasteth.

15There is gold, and a multitude of rubies;

But the lips of knowledge are a precious jewel.

[16]Take his garment that is surety for a stranger;

And hold him in pledge that is surety for an alien woman.

[17]Bread of falsehood is sweet to a man;

But afterwards his mouth shall be filled with gravel.

[18]Every purpose is established by counsel;

And with good advice carry on war.

[19]He that goeth about as a talebearer revealeth secrets;

Therefore meddle not with him that openeth wide his lips.

[20]Whoso curseth his father or his mother,

His lamp shall be put out in the blackest darkness.

[21]An estate may be gotten hastily at the beginning;

But the end thereof shall not be blessed.

[22]Say not thou: 'I will requite evil';

Wait for the Lord, and He will save thee.

[23]Divers weights are an abomination to the Lord;

And a false balance is not good.

[24]A man's goings are of the Lord;

How then can man look to his way?

[25]It is a snare to a man rashly to say: 'Holy',

And after vows to make inquiry.

[26]A wise king sifteth the wicked,

And turneth the wheel over them.

[27]The spirit of man is the lamp of the Lord,

Searching all the inward parts.

[28]Mercy and truth preserve the king;

And his throne is upheld by mercy.

[29]The glory of young men is their strength;

And the beauty of old men is the hoary head.

[30]Sharp wounds cleanse away evil;

So do stripes that reach the inward parts.

21

The king's heart is in the hand of the Lord, as the watercourses:

He turneth it whithersoever He will.

2Every way of a man is right in his own eyes;

But the Lord weigheth the hearts.

3To do righteousness and justice

Is more acceptable to the Lord than sacrifice.

4A haughty look, and a proud heart—

The tillage of the wicked is sin.

5The thoughts of the diligent tend only to plenteousness;

But every one that is hasty hasteth only to want.

6The getting of treasures by a lying tongue

Is a vapour driven to and fro; they [that seek them] seek death.

7The violence of the wicked shall drag them away;

Because they refuse to do justly.

8The way of man is froward and strange;

But as for the pure, his work is right.

9It is better to dwell in a corner of the housetop,

Than in a house in common with a contentious woman.

10The soul of the wicked desireth evil;

His neighbour findeth no favour in his eyes.

11When the scorner is punished, the thoughtless is made wise;

And when the wise is instructed, he receiveth knowledge.

12The Righteous One considereth the house of the wicked;

Overthrowing the wicked to their ruin.

13Whoso stoppeth his ears at the cry of the poor,

He also shall cry himself, but shall not be answered.

14A gift in secret pacifieth anger,

And a present in the bosom strong wrath.

15To do justly is joy to the righteous,

But ruin to the workers of iniquity.

[16]The man that strayeth out of the way of understanding

Shall rest in the congregation of the shades.

[17]He that loveth pleasure shall be a poor man;

He that loveth wine and oil shall not be rich.

[18]The wicked is a ransom for the righteous;

And the faithless cometh in the stead of the upright.

[19]It is better to dwell in a desert land,

Than with a contentious and fretful woman.

[20]There is desirable treasure and oil in the dwelling of the wise;

But a foolish man swalloweth it up.

[21]He that followeth after righteousness and mercy

Findeth life, prosperity, and honour.

[22]A wise man scaleth the city of the mighty,

And bringeth down the stronghold wherein it trusteth.

[23]Whoso keepeth his mouth and his tongue

Keepeth his soul from troubles.

[24]A proud and haughty man, scorner is his name,

Even he that dealeth in overbearing pride.

[25]The desire of the slothful killeth him;

For his hands refuse to labour.

[26]There is that coveteth greedily all the day long;

But the righteous giveth and spareth not.

[27]The sacrifice of the wicked is an abomination;

How much more, when he bringeth it with the proceeds of wickedness?

[28]A false witness shall perish;

But the man that obeyeth shall speak unchallenged.

[29]A wicked man hardeneth his face;

But as for the upright, he looketh well to his way.

[30]There is no wisdom nor understanding

Nor counsel against the Lord.

³¹The horse is prepared against the day of battle;

But victory is of the Lord.

22 A good name is rather to be chosen than great riches,

And loving favour rather than silver and gold.

²The rich and the poor meet together—

The Lord is the maker of them all.

³A prudent man seeth the evil, and hideth himself;

But the thoughtless pass on, and are punished.

⁴The reward of humility is the fear of the Lord,

Even riches, and honour, and life.

⁵Thorns and snares are in the way of the froward;

He that keepeth his soul holdeth himself far from them.

⁶Train up a child in the way he should go,

And even when he is old, he will not depart from it.

⁷The rich ruleth over the poor,

And the borrower is servant to the lender.

⁸He that soweth iniquity shall reap vanity;

And the rod of his wrath shall fail.

⁹He that hath a bountiful eye shall be blessed;

For he giveth of his bread to the poor.

¹⁰Cast out the scorner, and contention will go out;

Yea, strife and shame will cease.

¹¹He that loveth pureness of heart,

That hath grace in his lips, the king shall be his friend.

¹²The eyes of the Lord preserve him that hath knowledge,

But He overthroweth the words of the faithless man.

¹³The sluggard saith: 'There is a lion without;

I shall be slain in the streets.'

¹⁴The mouth of strange women is a deep pit:

He that is abhorred of the Lord shall fall therein.

¹⁵Foolishness is bound up in the heart of a child;

But the rod of correction shall drive it far from him.

¹⁶One may oppress the poor, yet will their gain increase;

One may give to the rich, yet will want come.

¹⁷Incline thine ear, and hear the words of the wise,

And apply thy heart unto my knowledge.

¹⁸For it is a pleasant thing if thou keep them within thee;

Let them be established altogether upon thy lips.

¹⁹That thy trust may be in the Lord,

I have made them known to thee this day, even to thee.

²⁰Have not I written unto thee excellent things

Of counsels and knowledge;

²¹That I might make thee know the certainty of the words of truth,

That thou mightest bring back words of truth to them that send thee?

²²Rob not the weak, because he is weak,

Neither crush the poor in the gate;

²³For the Lord will plead their cause,

And despoil of life those that despoil them.

²⁴Make no friendship with a man that is given to anger;

And with a wrathful man thou shalt not go;

²⁵Lest thou learn his ways,

And get a snare to thy soul.

²⁶Be thou not of them that strike hands,

Or of them that are sureties for debts;

²⁷If thou hast not wherewith to pay,

Why should he take away thy bed from under thee?

²⁸Remove not the ancient landmark,

Which thy fathers have set.

²⁹Seest thou a man diligent in his business? he shall stand before kings;

He shall not stand before mean men.

23When thou sittest to eat with a ruler,

Consider well him that is before thee;

²And put a knife to thy throat,

If thou be a man given to appetite.

³Be not desirous of his dainties;

Seeing they are deceitful food.

⁴Weary not thyself to be rich;

Cease from thine own wisdom. ⁵Wilt thou set thine eyes upon it? it is gone;

For riches certainly make themselves wings,

Like an eagle that flieth toward heaven.

⁶Eat thou not the bread of him that hath an evil eye,

Neither desire thou his dainties;

⁷For as one that hath reckoned within himself, so is he:

'Eat and drink', saith he to thee;

But his heart is not with thee.

⁸The morsel which thou hast eaten shalt thou vomit up,

And lose thy sweet words.

⁹Speak not in the ears of a fool;

For he will despise the wisdom of thy words.

¹⁰Remove not the ancient landmark;

And enter not into the fields of the fatherless;

¹¹For their Redeemer is strong;

He will plead their cause with thee.

¹²Apply thy heart unto instruction,

And thine ears to the words of knowledge.

¹³Withhold not correction from the child;

For though thou beat him with the rod, he will not die.

¹⁴Thou beatest him with the rod,

And wilt deliver his soul from the nether-world.

[15]My son, if thy heart be wise,

My heart will be glad, even mine;

[16]Yea, my reins will rejoice,

When thy lips speak right things.

[17]Let not thy heart envy sinners,

But be in the fear of the Lord all the day;

[18]For surely there is a future;

And thy hope shall not be cut off.

[19]Hear thou, my son, and be wise,

And guide thy heart in the way.

[20]Be not among winebibbers;

Among gluttonous eaters of flesh;

[21]For the drunkard and the glutton shall come to poverty;

And drowsiness shall clothe a man with rags.

[22]Hearken unto thy father that begot thee,

And despise not thy mother when she is old.

[23]Buy the truth, and sell it not;

Also wisdom, and instruction, and understanding.

[24]The father of the righteous will greatly rejoice;

And he that begetteth a wise child will have joy of him.

[25]Let thy father and thy mother be glad,

And let her that bore thee rejoice.

[26]My son, give me thy heart,

And let thine eyes observe my ways.

[27]For a harlot is a deep ditch;

And an alien woman is a narrow pit.

[28]She also lieth in wait as a robber,

And increaseth the faithless among men.

[29]Who crieth: 'Woe'? who: 'Alas'?

Who hath contentions? who hath raving?

Who hath wounds without cause?

Who hath redness of eyes?

³⁰They that tarry long at the wine;

They that go to try mixed wine.

³¹Look not thou upon the wine when it is red,

When it giveth its colour in the cup,

When it glideth down smoothly;

³²At the last it biteth like a serpent,

And stingeth like a basilisk.

³³Thine eyes shall behold strange things,

And thy heart shall utter confused things.

³⁴Yea, thou shalt be as he that lieth down in the midst of the sea,

Or as he that lieth upon the top of a mast.

³⁵'They have struck me, and I felt it not,

They have beaten me, and I knew it not;

When shall I awake? I will seek it yet again.'

24 Be not thou envious of evil men,

Neither desire to be with them.

²For their heart studieth destruction,

And their lips talk of mischief.

³Through wisdom is a house builded;

And by understanding it is established;

⁴And by knowledge are the chambers filled

With all precious and pleasant riches.

⁵A wise man is strong;

Yea, a man of knowledge increaseth strength.

⁶For with wise advice thou shalt make thy war;

And in the multitude of counsellors there is safety.

⁷Wisdom is as unattainable to a fool as corals;

He openeth not his mouth in the gate.

⁸He that deviseth to do evil,

Men shall call him a mischievous person.

⁹The thought of foolishness is sin;

And the scorner is an abomination to men.

¹⁰If thou faint in the day of adversity,

Thy strength is small indeed.

¹¹Deliver them that are drawn unto death;

And those that are ready to be slain wilt thou forbear to rescue?

¹²If thou sayest: 'Behold, we knew not this',

Doth not He that weigheth the hearts consider it?

And He that keepeth thy soul, doth not He know it?

And shall not He render to every man according to his works?

¹³My son, eat thou honey, for it is good,

And the honeycomb is sweet to thy taste;

¹⁴So know thou wisdom to be unto thy soul;

If thou hast found it, then shall there be a future,

And thy hope shall not be cut off.

¹⁵Lie not in wait, O wicked man, against the dwelling of the righteous,

Spoil not his resting-place;

¹⁶For a righteous man falleth seven times, and riseth up again,

But the wicked stumble under adversity.

¹⁷Rejoice not when thine enemy falleth,

And let not thy heart be glad when he stumbleth;

¹⁸Lest the Lord see it, and it displease Him,

And He turn away His wrath from him.

¹⁹Fret not thyself because of evil-doers,

Neither be thou envious at the wicked;

²⁰For there will be no future to the evil man,

The lamp of the wicked shall be put out.

²¹My son, fear thou the Lord and the king,

And meddle not with them that are given to change;

²²For their calamity shall rise suddenly;

And who knoweth the ruin from them both?

²³These also are sayings of the wise.

To have respect of persons in judgment is not good.

²⁴He that saith unto the wicked: 'Thou art righteous',

Peoples shall curse him, nations shall execrate him;

²⁵But to them that decide justly shall be delight,

And a good blessing shall come upon them.

²⁶He kisseth the lips

That giveth a right answer.

²⁷Prepare thy work without,

And make it fit for thyself in the field;

And afterwards build thy house.

²⁸Be not a witness against thy neighbour without cause;

And deceive not with thy lips.

²⁹Say not: 'I will do so to him as he hath done to me;

I will render to the man according to his work.'

³⁰I went by the field of the slothful,

And by the vineyard of the man void of understanding;

³¹And, lo, it was all grown over with thistles,

The face thereof was covered with nettles,

And the stone wall thereof was broken down.

³²Then I beheld, and considered well;

I saw, and received instruction.

³³'Yet a little sleep, a little slumber,

A little folding of the hands to sleep'—

³⁴So shall thy poverty come as a runner,

And thy want as an armed man.

25
These also are proverbs of Solomon, which the men of Hezekiah king of Judah copied out.

²It is the glory of God to conceal a thing;

But the glory of kings is to search out a matter.

³The heaven for height, and the earth for depth,

And the heart of kings is unsearchable.

⁴Take away the dross from the silver,

And there cometh forth a vessel for the refiner;

⁵Take away the wicked from before the king,

And his throne shall be established in righteousness.

⁶Glorify not thyself in the presence of the king,

And stand not in the place of great men;

⁷For better is it that it be said unto thee: 'Come up hither',

Than that thou shouldest be put lower in the presence of the prince,

Whom thine eyes have seen.

⁸Go not forth hastily to strive,

Lest thou know not what to do in the end thereof,

When thy neighbour hath put thee to shame.

⁹Debate thy cause with thy neighbour,

But reveal not the secret of another;

¹⁰Lest he that heareth it revile thee,

And thine infamy turn not away.

¹¹A word fitly spoken

Is like apples of gold in settings of silver.

¹²As an ear-ring of gold, and an ornament of fine gold,

So is a wise reprover upon an obedient ear.

¹³As the cold of snow in the time of harvest,

So is a faithful messenger to him that sendeth him;

For he refresheth the soul of his master.

¹⁴As vapours and wind without rain,

So is he that boasteth himself of a false gift.

¹⁵By long forbearing is a ruler persuaded,

And a soft tongue breaketh the bone.

¹⁶Hast thou found honey? eat so much as is sufficient for thee,

Lest thou be filled therewith, and vomit it.

¹⁷Let thy foot be seldom in thy neighbour's house;

Lest he be sated with thee, and hate thee.

¹⁸As a maul, and a sword, and a sharp arrow,

So is a man that beareth false witness against his neighbour.

¹⁹Confidence in an unfaithful man in time of trouble

Is like a broken tooth, and a foot out of joint.

²⁰As one that taketh off a garment in cold weather, and as vinegar upon nitre,

So is he that singeth songs to a heavy heart.

²¹If thine enemy be hungry, give him bread to eat,

And if he be thirsty, give him water to drink;

²²For thou wilt heap coals of fire upon his head,

And the Lord will reward thee.

²³The north wind bringeth forth rain,

And a backbiting tongue an angry countenance.

²⁴It is better to dwell in a corner of the housetop,

Than in a house in common with a contentious woman.

²⁵As cold waters to a faint soul,

So is good news from a far country.

²⁶As a troubled fountain, and a corrupted spring,

So is a righteous man that giveth way before the wicked.

²⁷It is not good to eat much honey;

So for men to search out their own glory is not glory.

²⁸Like a city broken down and without a wall,

So is he whose spirit is without restraint.

26 As snow in summer, and as rain in harvest,

So honour is not seemly for a fool.

²As the wandering sparrow, as the flying swallow,

So the curse that is causeless shall come home.

³A whip for the horse, a bridle for the ass,

And a rod for the back of fools.

⁴Answer not a fool according to his folly,

Lest thou also be like unto him.

⁵Answer a fool according to his folly,

Lest he be wise in his own eyes.

⁶He that sendeth a message by the hand of a fool

Cutteth off his own feet, and drinketh damage.

⁷The legs hang limp from the lame;

So is a parable in the mouth of fools.

⁸As a small stone in a heap of stones,

So is he that giveth honour to a fool.

⁹As a thorn that cometh into the hand of a drunkard,

So is a parable in the mouth of fools.

⁸As a small stone in a heap of stones,

So is he that giveth honour to a fool.

⁹As a thorn that cometh into the hand of a drunkard,

So is a parable in the mouth of fools.

¹⁰A master performeth all things;

But he that stoppeth a fool is as one that stoppeth a flood.

¹¹As a dog that returneth to his vomit,

So is a fool that repeateth his folly.

¹²Seest thou a man wise in his own eyes?

There is more hope of a fool than of him.

¹³The sluggard saith: 'There is a lion in the way;

Yea, a lion is in the streets.'

¹⁴The door is turning upon its hinges,

And the sluggard is still upon his bed.

¹⁵The sluggard burieth his hand in the dish;

It wearieth him to bring it back to his mouth.

¹⁶The sluggard is wiser in his own eyes

Than seven men that give wise answer.

¹⁷He that passeth by, and meddleth with strife not his own,

Is like one that taketh a dog by the ears.

¹⁸As a madman who casteth firebrands,

Arrows, and death;

¹⁹So is the man that deceiveth his neighbour,

And saith: 'Am not I in sport?'

²⁰Where no wood is, the fire goeth out;

And where there is no whisperer, contention ceaseth.

²¹As coals are to burning coals, and wood to fire;

So is a contentious man to kindle strife.

²²The words of a whisperer are as dainty morsels,

And they go down into the innermost parts of the body.

²³Burning lips and a wicked heart

Are like an earthen vessel overlaid with silver dross.

²⁴He that hateth dissembleth with his lips,

But he layeth up deceit within him.

²⁵When he speaketh fair,

Believe him not;

For there are seven abominations in his heart.

²⁶Though his hatred be concealed with deceit,

His wickedness shall be revealed before the congregation.

²⁷Whoso diggeth a pit shall fall therein;

And he that rolleth a stone, it shall return upon him.

²⁸A lying tongue hateth those that are crushed by it;

And a flattering mouth worketh ruin.

27 Boast not thyself of to-morrow;

For thou knowest not what a day may bring forth.

[2]Let another man praise thee, and not thine own mouth;

A stranger, and not thine own lips.

[3]A stone is heavy, and the sand weighty;

But a fool's vexation is heavier than they both.

[4]Wrath is cruel, and anger is overwhelming;

But who is able to stand before jealousy?

[5]Better is open rebuke

Than love that is hidden.

[6]Faithful are the wounds of a friend;

But the kisses of an enemy are importunate.

[7]The full soul loatheth a honeycomb;

But to the hungry soul every bitter thing is sweet.

[8]As a bird that wandereth from her nest,

So is a man that wandereth from his place.

[9]Ointment and perfume rejoice the heart;

So doth the sweetness of a man's friend by hearty counsel.

[10]Thine own friend, and thy father's friend, forsake not;

Neither go into thy brother's house in the day of thy calamity;

Better is a neighbour that is near than a brother far off.

[11]My son, be wise, and make my heart glad,

That I may answer him that taunteth me.

[12]A prudent man seeth the evil, and hideth himself;

But the thoughtless pass on, and are punished.

[13]Take his garment that is surety for a stranger;

And hold him in pledge that is surety for an alien woman.

[14]He that blesseth his friend with a loud voice, rising early in the morning,

It shall be counted a curse to him.

[15]A continual dropping in a very rainy day

And a contentious woman are alike;

[16]He that would hide her hideth the wind,

And the ointment of his right hand betrayeth itself.

¹⁷Iron sharpeneth iron;

So a man sharpeneth the countenance of his friend.

¹⁸Whoso keepeth the fig-tree shall eat the fruit thereof;

And he that waiteth on his master shall be honoured.

¹⁹As in water face answereth to face,

So the heart of man to man.

²⁰The nether-world and Destruction are never satiated;

So the eyes of man are never satiated.

²¹The refining pot is for silver, and the furnace for gold,

And a man is tried by his praise.

²²Though thou shouldest bray a fool in a mortar with a pestle among groats,

Yet will not his foolishness depart from him.

²³Be thou diligent to know the state of thy flocks,

And look well to thy herds;

²⁴For riches are not for ever;

And doth the crown endure unto all generations?

²⁵When the hay is mown, and the tender grass showeth itself,

And the herbs of the mountains are gathered in;

²⁶The lambs will be for thy clothing,

And the goats the price for a field.

²⁷And there will be goats' milk enough for thy food, for the food of thy household;

And maintenance for thy maidens.

28The wicked flee when no man pursueth;

But the righteous are secure as a young lion.

²For the transgression of a land many are the princes thereof;

But by a man of understanding and knowledge established order shall long continue.

³A poor man that oppresseth the weak

Is like a sweeping rain which leaveth no food.

⁴They that forsake the law praise the wicked;

But such as keep the law contend with them.

⁵Evil men understand not justice;

But they that seek the Lord understand all things.

⁶Better is the poor that walketh in his integrity,

Than he that is perverse in his ways, though he be rich.

⁷A wise son observeth the teaching;

But he that is a companion of gluttonous men shameth his father.

⁸He that augmenteth his substance by interest and increase,

Gathereth it for him that is gracious to the poor.

⁹He that turneth away his ear from hearing the law,

Even his prayer is an abomination.

¹⁰Whoso causeth the upright to go astray in an evil way,

He shall fall himself into his own pit;

But the whole-hearted shall inherit good.

¹¹The rich man is wise in his own eyes;

But the poor that hath understanding searcheth him through.

¹²When the righteous exult, there is great glory;

But when the wicked rise, men must be sought for.

¹³He that covereth his transgressions shall not prosper;

But whoso confesseth and forsaketh them shall obtain mercy.

¹⁴Happy is the man that feareth alway;

But he that hardeneth his heart shall fall into evil.

¹⁵As a roaring lion, and a ravenous bear;

So is a wicked ruler over a poor people.

¹⁶The prince that lacketh understanding is also a great oppressor;

But he that hateth covetousness shall prolong his days.

¹⁷A man that is laden with the blood of any person

Shall hasten his steps unto the pit; none will support him.

¹⁸Whoso walketh uprightly shall be saved;

But he that is perverse in his ways shall fall at once.

¹⁹He that tilleth his ground shall have plenty of bread;

But he that followeth after vain things shall have poverty enough.

²⁰A faithful man shall abound with blessings;

But he that maketh haste to be rich shall not be unpunished.

²¹To have respect of persons is not good;

For a man will transgress for a piece of bread.

²²He that hath an evil eye hasteneth after riches,

And knoweth not that want shall come upon him.

²³He that rebuketh a man shall in the end find more favour

Than he that flattereth with the tongue.

²⁴Whoso robbeth his father or his mother, and saith: 'It is no transgression',

The same is the companion of a destroyer.

²⁵He that is of a greedy spirit stirreth up strife;

But he that putteth his trust in the Lord shall be abundantly gratified.

²⁶He that trusteth in his own heart is a fool;

But whoso walketh wisely, he shall escape.

²⁷He that giveth unto the poor shall not lack;

But he that hideth his eyes shall have many a curse.

²⁸When the wicked rise, men hide themselves;

But when they perish, the righteous increase.

29 He that being often reproved hardeneth his neck

Shall suddenly be broken, and that without remedy.

²When the righteous are increased, the people rejoice;

But when the wicked beareth rule, the people sigh.

³Whoso loveth wisdom rejoiceth his father;

But he that keepeth company with harlots wasteth his substance.

⁴The king by justice establisheth the land;

But he that exacteth gifts overthroweth it.

⁵A man that flattereth his neighbour

Spreadeth a net for his steps.

⁶In the transgression of an evil man there is a snare;

But the righteous doth sing and rejoice.

⁷The righteous taketh knowledge of the cause of the poor;

The wicked understandeth not knowledge.

⁸Scornful men set a city in a blaze;

But wise men turn away wrath.

⁹If a wise man contendeth with a foolish man,

Whether he be angry or laugh, there will be no rest.

¹⁰The men of blood hate him that is sincere;

And as for the upright, they seek his life.

¹¹A fool spendeth all his spirit;

But a wise man stilleth it within him.

¹²If a ruler hearkeneth to falsehood,

All his servants are wicked.

¹³The poor man and the oppressor meet together;

The Lord giveth light to the eyes of them both.

¹⁴The king that faithfully judgeth the poor,

His throne shall be established for ever.

¹⁵The rod and reproof give wisdom;

But a child left to himself causeth shame to his mother.

¹⁶When the wicked are increased, transgression increaseth;

But the righteous shall gaze upon their fall.

¹⁷Correct thy son, and he will give thee rest;

Yea, he will give delight unto thy soul.

¹⁸Where there is no vision, the people cast off restraint;

But he that keepeth the law, happy is he.

¹⁹A servant will not be corrected by words;

For though he understand, there will be no response.

²⁰Seest thou a man that is hasty in his words?

There is more hope for a fool than for him.

²¹He that delicately bringeth up his servant from a child

Shall have him become master at the last.

²²An angry man stirreth up strife,

And a wrathful man aboundeth in transgression.

²³A man's pride shall bring him low;

But he that is of a lowly spirit shall attain to honour.

²⁴Whoso is partner with a thief hateth his own soul:

He heareth the adjuration and uttereth nothing.

²⁵The fear of man bringeth a snare;

But whoso putteth his trust in the Lord shall be set up on high.

²⁶Many seek the ruler's favour;

But a man's judgment cometh from the Lord.

²⁷An unjust man is an abomination to the righteous;

And he that is upright in the way is an abomination to the wicked.

30 The words of Agur the son of Jakeh; the burden.

The man saith unto Ithiel, unto Ithiel and Ucal:

²Surely I am brutish, unlike a man,

And have not the understanding of a man;

³And I have not learned wisdom,

That I should have the knowledge of the Holy One.

⁴Who hath ascended up into heaven, and descended?

Who hath gathered the wind in his fists?

Who hath bound the waters in his garment?

Who hath established all the ends of the earth?

What is his name, and what is his son's name, if thou knowest?

⁵Every word of God is tried;

He is a shield unto them that take refuge in Him.

⁶Add thou not unto His words,

Lest He reprove thee, and thou be found a liar.

[7]Two things have I asked of Thee;

Deny me them not before I die:

[8]Remove far from me falsehood and lies;

Give me neither poverty nor riches; feed me with mine allotted bread;

[9]Lest I be full, and deny, and say: 'Who is the Lord?'

Or lest I be poor, and steal,

And profane the name of my God.

[10]Slander not a servant unto his master,

Lest he curse thee, and thou be found guilty.

[11]There is a generation that curse their father,

And do not bless their mother.

[12]There is a generation that are pure in their own eyes,

And yet are not washed from their filthiness.

[13]There is a generation, Oh how lofty are their eyes!

And their eyelids are lifted up.

[14]There is a generation whose teeth are as swords, and their great teeth as knives,

To devour the poor from off the earth, and the needy from among men.

[15]The horseleech hath two daughters: 'Give, give.'

There are three things that are never satisfied,

Yea, four that say not: 'Enough':

[16]The grave; and the barren womb;

The earth that is not satisfied with water;

And the fire that saith not: 'Enough.'

[17]The eye that mocketh at his father,

And despiseth to obey his mother,

The ravens of the valley shall pick it out,

And the young vultures shall eat it.

[18]There are three things which are too wonderful for me,

Yea, four which I know not:

[19]The way of an eagle in the air;

The way of a serpent upon a rock;

The way of a ship in the midst of the sea;

And the way of a man with a young woman.

20So is the way of an adulterous woman;

She eateth, and wipeth her mouth,

And saith: 'I have done no wickedness.'

21For three things the earth doth quake,

And for four it cannot endure:

22For a servant when he reigneth;

And a churl when he is filled with food;

23For an odious woman when she is married;

And a handmaid that is heir to her mistress.

24There are four things which are little upon the earth,

But they are exceeding wise:

25The ants are a people not strong,

Yet they provide their food in the summer;

26The rock-badgers are but a feeble folk,

Yet make they their houses in the crags;

27The locusts have no king,

Yet go they forth all of them by bands;

28The spider thou canst take with the hands,

Yet is she in kings' palaces.

29There are three things which are stately in their march,

Yea, four which are stately in going:

30The lion, which is mightiest among beasts,

And turneth not away for any;

31The greyhound; the he-goat also;

And the king, against whom there is no rising up.

32If thou hast done foolishly in lifting up thyself,

Or if thou hast planned devices, lay thy hand upon thy mouth.

33For the churning of milk bringeth forth curd,

And the wringing of the nose bringeth forth blood;

So the forcing of wrath bringeth forth strife.

31
The words of king Lemuel; the burden wherewith his mother corrected him.

[2]What, my son? and what, O son of my womb?

And what, O son of my vows?

[3]Give not thy strength unto women,

Nor thy ways to that which destroyeth kings.

[4]It is not for kings, O [1]Lemuel, it is not for kings to drink wine:

Nor for princes to say: 'Where is strong drink?'

[5]Lest they drink, and forget that which is decreed,

And pervert the justice due to any that is afflicted.

[6]Give strong drink unto him that is ready to perish,

And wine unto the bitter in soul;

[7]Let him drink, and forget his poverty,

And remember his misery no more.

[8]Open thy mouth for the dumb,

In the cause of all such as are appointed to destruction.

[9]Open thy mouth, judge righteously,

And plead the cause of the poor and needy.

[10]אA woman of valour who can find?

For her price is far above rubies.

[11]בThe heart of her husband doth aafely trust in her,

And he hath no lack of gain.

[12]גShe doeth him good and not evil

All the days of her life.

[13]דShe seeketh wool and flax,

And worketh willingly with her hands.

[14]הShe is like the merchant-ships; She bringeth her food from afar.

[15]וShe riseth also while it is yet night,

And giveth food to her household,

And a portion to her maidens.

¹⁶ט She considereth a field, and buyeth it;

With the fruit of her hands she planteth a vineyard.

¹⁷ח She girdeth her loins with strength,

And maketh strong her arms.

¹⁸ט She perceiveth that her merchandise is good;

Her lamp goeth not out by night.

¹⁹י She layeth her hands to the distaff,

And her hands hold the spindle.

²⁰כ She stretcheth out her hand to the poor;

Yea, she reacheth forth her hands to the needy.

²¹ל She is not afraid of the snow for her household;

For all her household are clothed with scarlet.

²²מ She maketh for herself coverlets;

Her clothing is fine linen and purple.

²³נ Her husband is known in the gates,

When he sitteth among the elders of the land.

²⁴ס She maketh linen garments and selleth them;

And delivereth girdles unto the merchant.

²⁵ע Strength and dignity are her clothing;

And she laugheth at the time to come.

²⁶פ She openeth her mouth with wisdom;

And the law of kindness is on her tongue.

²⁷צ She looketh well to the ways of her household,

And eateth not the bread of idleness.

²⁸ק Her children rise up, and call her blessed;

Her husband also, and he praiseth her:

²⁹ר' Many daughters have done valiantly,

But thou excellest them all.'

30ש Grace is deceitful, and beauty is vain;

But a woman that feareth the Lord, she shall be praised.

31ת Give her of the fruit of her hands;

And let her works praise her in the gates.

69116781R00110